TREAD UPON THE LION

Tommie Titcombe with his helper, Joseph, one of the early baptized Yagba believers. Egbe, 1914.

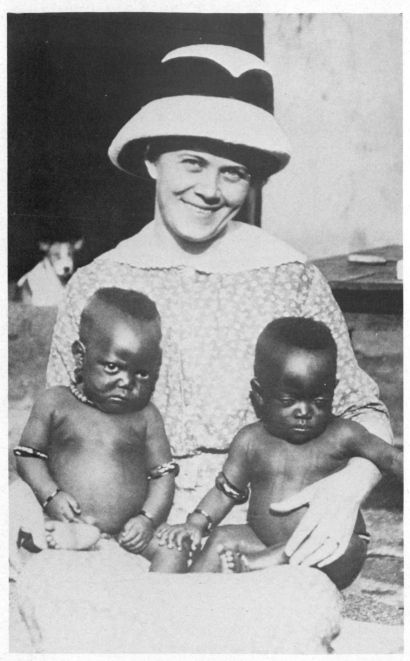

Ethel Titcombe with Reuben and Ruth, the first Yagba twins known to live, saved by her on Christmas Day 1915.

Tread upon the lion

The story of Tommie Titcombe

Sophie de la Haye

Tread upon the lion

The story of Tommie Titcombe

Published by SIM International

Designed and illustrated by Charles J. Guth

ISBN 0-919470-14-9
Library of Congress catalog number 73-91236
The Scriptures quoted under each chapter title are taken from the *New American Standard Bible* — 1960, 1962, 1963, 1968, 1971.
Used by permission of the Lockman Foundation.

SIM Offices

Australia: P.O. Box 371, Miranda, N.S.W.   2228
Canada: 10 Huntingdale Blvd., Scarborough, Ont.   M1W 2S5
Great Britain: Ullswater Cres., Coulsdon, Surrey   CR3 2HR
New Zealand: P.O. Box 38588, Howick
Singapore: Bras Basah, P.O. Box 239, Singapore   9118
Southern Africa: Private Bag 5, Westhoven
                    Johannesburg 2142, South Africa
Switzerland: Case Postale 42, 1000 Lausanne, 20 Sévelin
U.S.A.: P.O. Box 7900, Charlotte, NC   28217

First printing April 1974
Second printing October 1975
Third printing November 1980
Fourth printing April 1987

Printed in Canada

To: Tommie and Ethel's children:
     Clarence, Edith and Emerson
To: The ECWA Yoruba Church

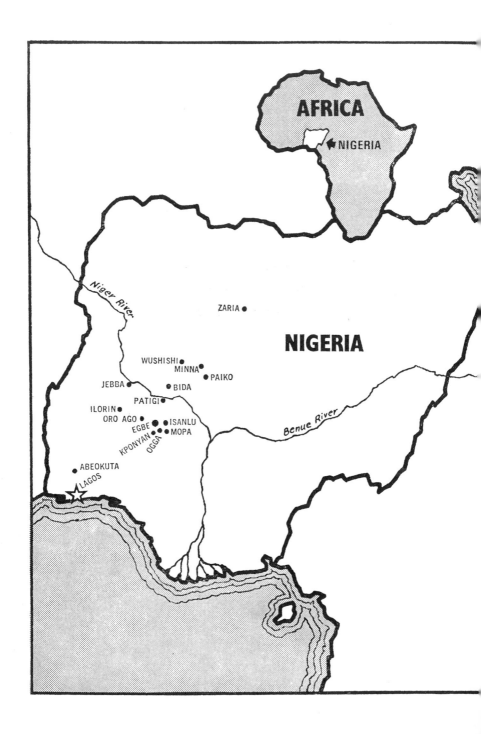

Contents

Foreword

There was only one Tommie Titcombe. Some things God makes a lot of; others just one of a kind. Africa, SIM, and a great host of men and women everywhere are grateful to God for His gift to the Church of this unusual man.

Tommie Titcombe was another example of God's delight in proving that man's measuring stick is often wrong. Tommie was short in stature, not impressive, not imposing, even somewhat gruff in his manner. His academic preparation was scanty even by the standards of his day, and his physique was not robust.

His qualities were his God-centered conviction that he was to share Christ with the people of Africa, and his readiness to face the unknown and the uncomfortable. There was no need for mechanical amplification of his voice —he could be heard clearly at great distances. Though many times he was fearful, he did not falter or fail to prove God and hold Him true to His promises.

I am delighted and honored to introduce to you this gentleman and his faithful companion, Ethel. Their story as related by Sophie de la Haye is a gracious glimpse into the lives of two of God's choice children.

The last time I saw Tommie Titcombe was in the hospital, three weeks before he went to heaven. He was weary and weak, but greeted me with a smile and strong handshake. We chatted about his condition and his expectation to soon see Christ and many Yagba friends of long ago. To him it was the next and natural stage in life, to move on.

Then he grasped my hand and drew me closer. His eyes looked into mine as he said, "Ray, I've told you many times that long ago God gave me Psalm ninety-one as my special portion of Scripture. There are thirty-three promises in that psalm, and God has fulfilled every one of them for me, most of them many times."

He lay back on his pillow, exhausted, and I whispered a prayer briefly. As I left the room, I said, "Tommie, you have been a great example and inspiration to me. God bless you, and reward you."

He opened his eyes a bit and said, "He has, and He will. I'll see you up there."

Raymond J. Davis, D.D.
SIM General Director

Preface

I was an undergraduate English major at the University of British Columbia in Vancouver, Canada, and active in the Inter-Varsity Christian Fellowship chapter on campus, when Tommie Titcombe confronted me with the relevance of Jesus Christ's command, "Go . . . make disciples . . . and I will be with you. . . ."

We called him "TNT"—this small "giant" of a man. The Holy Spirit used his dynamic challenge to electrify audiences. He spoke for a verdict, and you either told the Lord you were available, or you weren't!

I had already invited Jesus Christ to take control of my life, but through Tommie, I gained direction. It was to be West Africa under SIM.

I am grateful for the privilege of preparing this book. It is not an exhaustive biography, but an effort to share with today's youth how God used one of their peers in *his* generation.

In weaving the tapestry of Tommie's life, I chose the promises of Psalm 91, his favorite, as the strong warp threads, for God made them good to him, one by one. Then I selected colorful strands from tapes, letters, diaries, eye witness accounts, and memories of family and friends at home and among Yoruba Christians, to highlight his experiences.

I have deliberately left untold much of the "past that is dead," but have included certain true happenings only because ECWA (Evangelical Churches of West Africa) in Yorubaland is what it is today because God sent Tommie to them.

It is my deep desire that God will use this record to challenge you, for as one of Nigeria's outstanding writers, Chinua Achebe, said:

"What is meaningful is what takes into account the past *and* the present. There are people who say forget the past. Well, you can't, because the present comes out of it. At the same time, you do not want to be mesmerized or immobilized by your contemplation of the past to the exclusion of what is happening today. The most meaningful work that African writers can do today will take into account our whole history: how we got here, and what it is today; and that will help us map out our plans for the future."*

I am deeply grateful to Dr. Raymond J. Davis, General Director of SIM, close friend and co-worker since Hausa language school days 36 years ago, for the privilege of preparing this biography and for making available to me all he'd written about Tommie.

It was Dr. Davis's desire for you to share the inspiration of Tommie's life that prompted him. I know had time permitted, he would have authored this book himself.

I sincerely thank friends who prayed; all who provided source material; Mr. Kerry Lovering, SIM Publications Secretary; Mr. Chuck Guth, staff artist; Miss Christine Ferrier, for careful and invaluable research; my husband, Ray, for inspiration and helps; my daughter Joy, and my friend, Mrs. Marjorie Phelps, for typing the manuscript.

It is my prayer that the Holy Spirit will use this record of Tommie's exploits for Jesus, his simple faith and dedication, to encourage you to present your body and the control of your life to the Lord Jesus Christ, to go anywhere with Him.

Sophie W. de la Haye
October 1973

* "Achebe: Accountable to His Society" Interview by Ernest and Pat Emenyonu. *Africa Report*, May 1972, page 25. By permission.

PART ONE

God's man for Yagbaland

1. Rain on the roof

"And he prayed again, and the sky poured rain . . ." James 5:18

Crowds of villagers danced and swayed around the foot of a tall palm tree, stamping and chanting to the throbbing drumbeat and piercing blast of rams' horns.

For weeks the people had been restless; the rains were late. Twice they had planted seed; twice it had died. Now something would happen —Daeke, the Shango priest, had promised rain.

Tommie recalled the situation clearly:

I had awakened early that morning and lay listening to excited voices and the sound of hurrying feet. I was inquisitive enough to get up and join the stragglers to see what was happening. The tall grass, burnt

1

brown in the scorching sun, rustled as I brushed through it on the narrow trail.

The drums stirred the crowd as they felt the insistent rhythm. Listening, they were glad. Surely they'd get rain now.

As I approached, I saw the people with their eyes fastened on the wiry figure of Daeke climbing to the treetop. He made a bed in its crown and sat down cross-legged.

"What are you doing up there?" I shouted.

"I'm getting as near to Shango as I can. He's going to give us rain."

Then I caught a glimpse of Daeke's big wooden idol sitting in a clearing close by. Near it a calf lay tethered, waiting.

The priest began calling on Shango; the people around me shouted and screamed; the music thundered on. If ever I saw a picture of the biblical account of Mount Carmel, I saw it then. There they were, in a frenzy, crying out to their god for rain.

We missionaries, living about 500 yards away, didn't get much sleep the next few nights, for they continued around the clock.

On the fourth day I walked over to ask Daeke, "Where's the rain?"

"Oh, white man, it's coming!"

The next morning he climbed down, sacrificed the calf, and sprinkled blood on the idol. But they had danced, cried, pleaded and sacrificed in vain. The rain didn't come.

Then the Muslims took over. They practically quoted Psalm 115.

"Sure, idols don't answer, they're made of wood and stone. They have eyes, but they're blind; they have ears, but they're deaf; they have mouths, but they're dumb. Allah will send rain."

They ordered a week-long fast; then, night and day, intoned their prayers: "*Allahu akbar! Allahu akbar! La ilaha, illa Allahu, Muhammad rasul Allah!*" "God is great! God is great! There is no God but God, and Muhammad is His prophet."

At the end of the week they went down to the river and sacrificed a ram. But the rain didn't come.

The animists tried; the Muslims tried; yet I'd said nothing to the Christians. But on the next Sunday afternoon after the message, David, the pastor, turned and said, "Isn't it time for us who belong to Jesus to pray for rain?"

Oh, I'd waited for this. I wouldn't suggest it as I wanted them to bring it up. "But David," I said, "the animists spent five days pleading for rain!"

"Yes, we know."

"What about the Muslims?"

That stumped him for a moment, then all of a sudden he said, "Yes, Muhammad lived and died." Then clapping his hands he said, "Oh, Pa, that's the difference!"

"What do you mean?"

"The Lord Jesus lived and died, but He came out of the grave. And He said, 'All authority has been given to me in heaven and on earth'."

"Well, David, what Bible promise shall we claim?"

Without a moment's hesitation he turned to James 5:17, 18 and read: "Elias was a man subject to like passions as we are, and he prayed earnestly that it might not rain: and it rained not on the earth by the space of three years and six months. And he prayed again, and the heaven gave rain, and the earth brought forth her fruit."

I turned to the congregation of more than a thousand people, who'd been following our dialogue with great enjoyment, and said, "Tomorrow night at seven, we're going to pray for rain. Come, if you believe God answers prayer." Then we dismissed.

Later, while relaxing on the veranda with David, I heard the drum beat out the message: "Now we'll see whose God lives. The Christians are going to ask their God for rain."

The next day was a scorcher. At 7 p.m. the church bell rang. It was a beautiful starlit night, not a cloud in the sky upon which to hang our faith; all we had were the promises of God.

My fellow-missionaries and I picked up our kerosene lanterns and headed for the church. In the yard we found the animists grouped on one side, and the Muslims on the other.

As I entered a small side door and mounted the platform, I thrilled to see the building packed. Lanterns here and there lit up eager faces and revealed the aisles filled with broad-brimmed umbrella hats.

"Why did you bring those hats?" I asked.

"Haven't we come to pray for rain? We'll need them going home."

I read James 5:17, 18 to them, then we all got down on our knees and began to pray, one after the other. "Lord, send rain. Lord, we need rain. Glorify your name in Yagbaland!"

We prayed five minutes, ten minutes, fifteen, then a groan went up all over the church. Twenty minutes, twenty-five passed. We heard a gentle tapping on the pan roof. The building was just four walls with a galvanized iron roof and no ceiling. Then we heard a pinging sound as the drops fell faster. Before long the downpour drowned out the voices

B

of those praying. We couldn't hear anything but the roar of the rain on the roof as God released torrents upon us.

As one man we stood to our feet, shouting for joy, and singing praises to our God, who lives and answers prayer.

The churchyard was empty when we started home; the onlookers hadn't brought their umbrella hats!

2. Plans for a future

"For I know the plans that I have for you, declares the Lord, plans for welfare and not for calamity to give you a future and a hope." Jeremiah 29:11

When Tommie Titcombe entered the Gospel Tabernacle in Hamilton, Canada, on Thanksgiving Day 1906, he didn't realize he was triggering God's plan for his life. By making a right decision that day, he began to be the answer to the prayers of a small group of Yagba Christians in far-off Nigeria, on Africa's West Coast:

A generation before Tommie's birth, during Africa's dark night of slavery, Daniel Onisanaiye was born of Yagba parents in the tiny village of Ogga, 300 miles north of Lagos, Nigeria's main port of entry.

One midnight the village of Ogga slept in the silvery silence of a full moon. A dog barked. There was a shout, then the firing of flintlocks. The villagers, startled awake, knew that slavery or death awaited them if the raiders caught them. Only those who reached the jungle had a chance to escape. In the confusion, parents roused their children; the children sobbed, tearful and bewildered.

Young Dani, running toward the undergrowth at the edge of the village, looked back to see his parents killed. He turned into the jungle, his bare feet feeling for the trail. His eyes adjusted to the friendly darkness as he hurried away, hoping that no one had noticed him.

But he didn't escape. The slavers caught him, chained him to the other captives and drove him down the trail to the slave market at Abeokuta. Little Dani suffered as he trotted to keep up with the rest. Thirsty in the blazing sun, and hungry, but most of all feeling sad and lonely, he wondered what would happen to him.

At Abeokuta, he was sold to a ruthless man who used him without mercy day in and day out, wet season and dry season, year after year.

Dani grew to manhood and was able to redeem himself from slavery. In time, he made his way down to Lagos, on the coast, and took up the trade of painting. He responded to the gospel, and began to attend Araromi Baptist Church, led by Dr. Agbebi. He learned to read, and bought a Yoruba Bible, which he understood because the Yagbas are a division of the Yoruba people. He became a master painter, married, owned his own home, and had a son. His roots went down deep in Lagos, but not deep enough to keep him there.

As he studied the Word, God gave him an overwhelming desire to go back to his birthplace to share the gospel with his own people, for missionaries hadn't reached his village yet. His wife and son tried every argument to keep him from going, but God was carrying out His great plan to reach Yagbaland. Dani's return was the first step.

So in 1904, three years after Sir Frederick Lugard became the first High Commissioner of the Protectorate of Northern Nigeria, Dani left the comforts of Lagos and returned to his home village, now safe from intertribal warfare and slave raids.

Back at Ogga, he found himself a stranger, but an elderly man, Adeniyi, befriended him. When Dani showed him a Bible picture of the birth of Christ, Adeniyi excitedly pointed to the angels, saying he'd seen sparkling white creatures like them in a vision a few days before.

He concluded that Dani's message and book were true, and welcomed him into his home. The villagers, however, didn't greet him so cordially. His ways and conversation didn't conform to village life. They knew there was a Supreme Being whom they called *Olorun*, but he was faraway and unreal. On the other hand, *Esu* dogged them constantly. Fear of Satan's power dominated their daily lives. They spent their strength and wealth appeasing him at the whim of his representative, the witch doctor.

Dani came talking of a God who loved them, who had sent His Son to die for them. He explained that if they received Jesus as their Lord and Savior, they would be freed from the power of Satan, and from the bondage of fear. He was the first Christian they had ever seen, and he brought a black thing he called the *Holy Bible*, from which he read sweet words in their language.

Life had gone on in the same pattern for generations; this new teaching made the old men wary. But God encouraged Dani to sit down each afternoon under a shade tree and read aloud a portion from the Bible. The old ones rejected it, but young men paused to listen. Some drifted away, others returned to hear more. A few became Christians.

In 1901, the Sudan Interior Mission, then known as the Africa Industrial Mission, sent a party of four young men up the Niger River to Lokoja, where the Niger meets the Benue. Early in 1902 they opened their first station, among the Nupes, at Patigi, 160 miles farther up the Niger, on the southern bank. Dani and the handful of young men who now followed Christ didn't know that missionaries were living about 50 miles through the forest, but they began to pray that God would send one to help them.

In June 1905, Mr. E. F. Lang made a long trek into Yagbaland. By using a Yoruba-speaking Nupe carrier as interpreter, Mr. Lang shared the gospel from village to village. He was well received everywhere. One day he entered Ogga, to find the old man reading aloud to a group of young men from a Yoruba Bible. He could hardly believe his eyes.

Later, Mr. Lang heard Dani's miracle story from Dani himself. There was little sleep that night as the recent converts eagerly questioned the missionary about the new way. They asked for help. As Mr. Lang left, he urged them to pray that God would send His man.

The next year Mr. Lang returned. At Ogga he found that the older ones had refused to give their daughters to marry the young believers. But some of the girls, now believers, said they would marry only Christians. Mr. Lang reported: "A number ask for baptism . . . and one man says he has heard the Word, and something in his heart tells him to go and tell others."

The women of Ogga had a reputation far and wide for making the best earthenware pots available. People would walk many miles to Ogga market to buy pottery. Now men and women came seeking news about something new going on there. Word had traveled down the trails that Ogga had received the white man's religion and Book. Inquirers came to hear the truth.

Several times, believers from the village walked to Patigi for help. They were urged to pray. On one of his treks into Yagbaland, Mr. Lang took along some Yoruba alphabet cards and primers to encourage the young people to learn to read.

Early in 1907, Mr. Lang married Miss Schofield. It was their hope to go to Yagbaland. In November, however, Mrs. Lang was invalided home. She died in premature childbirth on board the S.S. *Falaba* en route to Liverpool, and was buried at sea. The baby, taken to Toronto, Canada, died a few months later.

Mr. Lang, who had remained at Patigi, spent Christmas with the believers at Ogga. The SIM Annual Report for that year included a touching note about this visit just before he left for furlough: "Mr. Lang appealed to them to let Jesus Christ come in and rule in their lives. The whole band of disciples rose to express their willingness to surrender their lives to Jesus Christ. When the missionary bade them goodbye, they parted with tears."

But God did not forget them; He was planning to answer their prayers within a year.

God had begun to prepare His messenger on September 17, 1881, when Tommie, the first of five children, was born to George and Sarah Titcombe in the small railroad town of Swindon, Wiltshire, England. Tommie's father, who worked as a laborer for the Great Western Railway, died while the children were young. After completing elementary school, Tommie, realizing his responsibilities as the oldest child, went to work in the railway shop as an apprentice molder. Laboring from six in the morning to ten o'clock at night, he earned the equivalent of $1.25 a week to help provide for the family.

At age 21, Tommie, though short in stature, was a sturdy, good-looking young man with wavy brown hair and mischievous blue eyes that gave away his love of fun and practical jokes. His animated, outgoing personality drew new friends easily. One day, when he was almost through his apprenticeship, he and several companions were caught in a rainstorm. They took shelter in the Salvation Army barracks where a meeting was in progress.

Tommie listened to the message and became deeply convicted of sin. Some days later at work, one of his friends, Bert Cox, a member of the Railway Mission, invited him to attend a prayer meeting. There, the two ladies in charge, Miss Caswell and Miss Cowie, explained the way of salvation to him. In his testimony, Tommie later would say, "Not many minutes after that, I knew I was saved for time and eternity."

In 1903, when Tommie was 22, he and two friends, George Cole and Bert Cox, pooled their resources and to their happy amazement found they had enough to pay passage for all three to Canada. There, Tommie found work at his trade in Hamilton, Ontario. Soon he joined the Gospel Tabernacle, pastored by Rev. P. W. Philpott. He taught Sunday School there and took part in street meetings. Apart from his work, Tommie's activities centered around the church, where there were many other young people. Strangely enough to those who knew him in later years, at this time he was reserved and shy.

On Thanksgiving Day 1906, at the morning service, Tommie heard missionary Charles Waddell, home on his first furlough from the work of SIM in Nigeria. Mr. Waddell challenged the young men to take the gospel to those who had never heard. That evening, Rev. Herbert Mackenzie, a visiting pastor from Cleveland, Ohio, spoke and at the close invited young people to dedicate their lives to Christ. Some sixty responded, Tommie among them.

The following day he told Mr. Philpott, "I received such a vision yesterday of the multitudes going into a Christless eternity, I felt I *must* answer the call." They discussed the need of Bible training.

Having heard, through missionary Charles Waddell, that SIM needed young men, Tommie asked for an interview with the Director, Rev. Rowland V. Bingham, in Toronto.

Years later, Mr. Bingham reminisced about that interview: "When Tommie first came I turned him down. His home history was not so unusual. He had been sole support of a widowed mother and had been compelled to leave school at an early age. In my first interview I outlined a comprehensive program of preparation that would require several years of study. When I bowed him out of my office, I thought I had seen the last of him."

But now that Tommie had a goal in life, he refused to be discouraged. With Pastor Philpott's help, in two weeks he was on his way to Dr. A. B. Simpson's Missionary Training Institute in New York City. During the year, he studied the Bible and related subjects diligently.

In the summer of 1907, he took a job as companion to an elderly gentleman. Tommie had the joy of leading the old man to Christ. In the autumn, this man's son, seeing potential in his father's happy young friend, made an attractive business offer to Tommie; but he, convinced that God wanted him in Africa, refused firmly. "Thank you, sir, but I am going back to Bible School and to Africa."

Tommie found the second year at the Missionary Training Institute more difficult. He worked hard to make the grade. He graduated, however, and back home he told his friends, "When I left the school, all the students gathered outside and sang me off to Africa."

Back in Canada, Tommie arranged for another interview with Mr. Bingham. Bingham turned him down again. Perplexed, Tommie nevertheless refused to give up. Telling of this interview some time later, Tommie said, "I told Mr. Bingham I was sorry he turned me down, because I had hoped to go out under SIM. But, if not SIM, no matter, I was going to Africa."

"What board are you going under, Mr. Titcombe?"

"I don't know, Mr. Bingham. It may be some old woman's washboard, but I'm going to Africa!"

"But where are you going to get your money?"

"I don't know, Mr. Bingham. That's God's business, not mine!"

Tommie, being a determined person, had surmounted many obstacles. He felt sad that the Mission had turned him down again.

Tommie told his pastor he'd not been accepted. Mr. Philpott sought to console him by promising to find him a church. Tommie refused the kind offer. "No, I don't want a church. The Lord has called me to Africa, and I'm going."

Pastor Philpott looked at him intently. Putting his hand on Tommie's head, he said, "Tommie, we're a poor church and I'm sorry we can't support you. However, we will pray for you." He announced from the pulpit the next Sunday that Tommie was going to Africa and urged the people to pray for him.

When Mr. Bingham realized that Tommie was determined to go, and that Pastor Philpott and his church were standing by Tommie in prayer, he relented and accepted him into SIM.

Thinking back to this event, Mr. Bingham said, "I used to be quite fearful of turning down one whom God had called, but I have long since learned that he will turn up again. Two years after my first meeting with Tommie, he called on me again. He had completed the course I had outlined for him and later on we decided to accept him. It was not easy to obtain men for the dangerous and difficult task of opening up this great, new country, so he went forth with little thought of the great career before him."

Just before Tommie left Canada, he heard furloughing SIM missionary Fred Lang tell about the group of young believers in Ogga praying that God would send a missionary to their tribe. Tommie wondered if God was sending him to help them.

Now accepted, Tommie enthusiastically assembled his outfit. He spent about $60. Friends shared their possessions. One lady gave him some plates; another, two cups and saucers. Still another bought herself new cutlery, and gave Tommie two knives, forks, and spoons from her old set. He bought a camp cot, bedding, and a few extra clothes, and packed them with some books in a small trunk. When Mr. Bingham booked passage for Tommie and George Sanderson, a graduate of Toronto Bible College, they had only half of their passage money. But before their departure, God provided as He promised.

After a commissioning service in July 1908, Tommie and George left by train for Montreal. There they boarded a ship for Liverpool.

After two weeks in England, Tommie needed money. The Lord didn't forget him. His friends at the Railway Mission gave a generous gift, and Tommie and George bought passage on an Elder Dempster mail boat going to West Africa.

In 1908 the West Coast of Africa was called "the white man's grave"; few who ventured there survived the climate and tropical fevers. As the boat slipped away from the dock in Liverpool, the band played, "Goodbye, we'll never see you again," and for many on board it would be true.

Life on shipboard wasn't too congenial. No sooner had they cleared the Mersey River than Tommie and George realized the kind of men they'd be living with for the next three weeks. The majority left restraint behind and drank continually. In disembarking to visit ports along the way, several fell into the sea and had to be fished out with boat hooks.

Tommie's cabin-mate used vile language. Tried to the limit one day, Tommie challenged him, "Sir, you insult my best friend."

"Your friend?" the man replied. "I have insulted your friend? Who is he? I don't even know his name."

"You certainly have! You've blasphemed the name of Jesus Christ. He is my Savior!"

"Are you a missionary?" the man sneered.

"Yes, I am."

"Are you going to work among those———?"

Tommie was furious. Squaring his shoulders he looked the man straight in the eye, "Yes, I am, and I consider it a privilege." Though Tommie was small, the fire in his eyes must have impressed the man, for he didn't offend in that way the remainder of the journey.

Tommie's excitement grew as the ship entered tropical waters and Africa's coastline came into view. With the Cape Verde Islands behind, as far as his eye could see the surf pounded against dazzling white sand, broken occasionally by a river emptying into the Atlantic, all against a backdrop of dense green jungle and cloudless blue sky. Time passed quickly now as he and George spent their days on deck.

Tommie never tired of gazing into the blue-green depths as the ship cut its way through the sea. The balmy nights were sheer magic; their blackness broken only by the reflection of the ship's lights on the water and the diamond-studded sky above. With his back against the rail at the stern, away off to the right, low on the horizon, he could see the Southern Cross. On moonlit nights he stayed out late, watching the ever-changing beauty of the tropical darkness.

At Freetown, Sierra Leone, the ship anchored offshore. In no time a fleet of small dugouts headed toward it. Laughing and gesticulating, the young Africans dove into the water after money thrown by the passengers, coming up with the coins held securely between their teeth.

Tommie and George waited their turn to disembark. With two others, they stepped into a "mammy chair" on the deck. This slinglike contraption, open on each side, had two-place seats for passengers to sit facing each other, knee-to-knee. A crane hoisted it up over the rail and lowered it to a waiting surf boat, rising and falling on the huge swell. Safely transferred to the boat, they were rowed to the dock.

On African soil for the first time, they mingled with multitudes of black people. A great longing welled up in Tommie's heart to tell them of God's love for them; but he couldn't bridge the language barrier.

Next they stopped in Gold Coast (now Ghana). Here again, Tommie saw throngs of Africans but couldn't communicate.

A few days later the ship reached the Niger River delta. Tommie and his fellow-missionary, with their luggage, went ashore on a government landing barge.

They spent a week trying to find a way up the river. In Burutu, an employee of a trading concern took pity on them and arranged that they board a company launch. Tommie had only $10 in his pocket. An ordinary man might have been tempted to worry, but as future days proved, this was no ordinary man.

PART TWO

Tommie tells it like it was
1908-1930

3. Under the shadow of the Almighty

"He who dwells in the shelter of the Most High will abide in the shadow of the Almighty."Psalm 91:1

The dark green, turgid river slid slowly by. I stood in the bow of the launch peering into the darkening night. The slow, rhythmic thump of the engine seemed strange in this new and different world. Soon we'd be forced to stop for the night as twilight is short in the tropics. Over there just a few hundred yards was the river bank—Africa, the land to which God had brought me. Strange sights, strange sounds, strange people! Not only were those on the shore part of another world; those on the boat seemed another breed, even though the color of their skin was the same as mine. I wondered what had brought them here. However, I was glad to be on my way up the Niger River at last, making progress toward my longed-for destination, the interior of this vast continent. Day after day for most of a week the launch pushed against the current, making almost imperceptible progress. Each bend of the river brought new sights. There were crocodiles whose noonday naps in the blazing sun we interrupted as we passed. Hippopotami continued their water games and swam uncomfortably close, investigating the noisy intruder. Every moment brought exciting new prospects as we glided past jungle, tall grass, picture-book scenes of tiny villages, canoes, and fishermen.

When we reached the confluence of the Niger and Benue Rivers at Lokoja, the captain asked us to disembark. His Excellency, the Governor of Nigeria, was boarding at this point. Other passengers couldn't travel when he and his party needed the ship. The Lord helped us overcome obstacles before; I knew He would now.

The Governor's party went aboard. But since the boat wasn't government property, concession was made and we passengers were allowed to ride on a barge towed behind. The journey upriver continued.

We dropped anchor at Mureji, a small trading post where the Niger and Kaduna Rivers meet. Here I said goodbye to my fellow missionary, George Sanderson, who would continue upstream as he was to be stationed at Wushishi. I stepped into a small dugout that came alongside to take me and my small trunk to the opposite bank.

I looked up at the brown-skinned boatman at the rear of the canoe, standing tall on a projecting wooden platform. He skillfully piloted me across the river, our goal the SIM station at Patigi. As we neared the shore I saw a white man waving. Drawing closer, I realized he must be Dr. Stirrett, a medical doctor, who, at 36, had sold his pharmacy and gone to Africa. Mr. Bingham had told him he was too old, but he went anyway, believing that God was sending him. Now, a few years later, Dr. Stirrett was the Mission's appointed leader in Nigeria.

There he stood, a short, bearded man wearing a huge pith helmet. He shouted, "Pull off your shoes and socks, brother!"

I removed more than that. I took off my pants, too, and waded ashore through the muddy water. On land and redressed, I experienced something that no man had ever done to me before. Dr. Stirrett put his arms around me and kissed me on both cheeks. He had long whiskers, and I didn't appreciate this sign of affection at all. But deep down in my heart

I was thankful to meet this man of whom I'd heard so much back in Canada.

We walked single file down the path cut through tropical trees and thick undergrowth. As the doctor talked, I was aware of new sights, smells, and sounds: vines hanging from trees I'd never seen before, the strong sweet scent of flowers and fruit, and the wild cacophany of bird calls. I thrilled to be approaching Patigi, three miles from the river.

As we entered the mission compound through an opening in the mud, thatch-topped fence, I saw about a dozen buildings, some round, others rectangular. We headed for the largest: red sun-dried brick walls, thatch-roofed like all the others, but in front of the door someone had planted exotic bougainvillaea, hibiscus and other tropical flowers. Stepping out of the glare and heat into the high-ceilinged sitting room, my first impression was of a strong, acrid odor.

"What's that smell?" I asked.

"Oh, probably the bats. Look up!"

I glanced up to see bats hanging head-down from the thatched roof like clusters of grapes. I wondered why he didn't get rid of them.

My next thought was food. I'd had no dinner; in fact I had eaten nothing since early morning, and I was ravenous. When we sat down at the table, a young African set a large enamel bowl before us. There was our supper; slices of cold yam swimming in a thick, reddish liquid.

"Yam and palm oil," Dr. Stirrett told me.

Hungry as I was, I didn't relish it.

At bedtime, Dr. Stirrett showed me my bed and explained about the mosquito net, already tucked under the bedding for the night. This net is supposed to keep mosquitoes out and let the air in. This one kept the air out and let the mosquitoes in. With a few safety pins I fixed it so I could get some sleep. I felt apprehensive, for every now and then I heard something like raindrops on the top of the net. It wasn't raining outside, so I realized it was the bats. They had come alive in the darkness.

As I lay trying to go to sleep, I heard other unusual sounds. "Dr. Stirrett, what's that?" I exclaimed.

"Oh," he said in a matter-of-fact voice, "that's probably just lizards. Watch!"

He reached for a shoe and tossed it across the room. It struck the chicken wire nailed over the window space. The lizards hanging on the outside plopped to the ground and skittered away.

I slept some, but wakened frequently. The whir of bat wings, the humming of mosquitoes patrolling around my net, and the night lizards silhouetted in the windows made me uncomfortable. I welcomed the morning, even though I wasn't rested. And that bed was the three season variety—no spring!

It was Sunday. As I crawled out of the mosquito net and looked across the room, I saw Dr. Stirrett's bed empty. I dressed hurriedly, and, stepping outside, met the doctor returning from the town. Breakfast was prominent in my mind, so I was glad he suggested we sit down. The cook brought the same dish used the previous night, and set it on the table between us.

"Today is Sunday and we light no fires," the doctor said as he observed my expression.

That was it. After thanks, I lifted the lid to see what we had for breakfast. Cold Guinea corn porridge covered with red palm oil. It really didn't look appetizing, but since I was hungry I thought to myself, "If this is breakfast, I'd better start."

I tried, but the grit in the porridge set my teeth on edge. Breakfast over, we engaged in morning devotions and then left for a service in a village six miles away. I perspired as we walked along the winding, sandy pathway. I still wore my travel clothes—most unsuitable for this climate.

On our return, Dr. Stirrett called the lad to bring our dinner. There it was—the same dish—cold yams and red palm oil. My hunger overcame my disappointment, so I ate what I could. Glancing around the room, I noticed a mailbag. Since Dr. Stirrett didn't mention it, I asked about it.

"I don't open mail on Sunday," he replied. He was a strict Scottish Presbyterian; that seemed too strict for me.

We rested during the heat of the day, and as evening drew on, Dr. Stirrett told me he never ate on Sunday evening. Consequently, neither did I.

Somehow, I survived my second night. The next morning I lost no time getting to the breakfast table.

"I don't have breakfast Monday mornings," he replied to the question on my face. So I didn't either.

Monday noon I enjoyed my first hot meal—yams and palm oil—although I'd been there since Saturday. I ate heartily after a 24-hour fast. We left some of that meal, so ate it for supper, too.

One day I went to market and couldn't resist buying a chicken. Dr. Stirrett wouldn't eat it, although he drank some soup. I was embarrassed to be enjoying the chicken in front of him, so resolved to conform. In time, I adjusted to his Spartan menu, varied now and then with porridge instead of yams.

Many things bothered me, but apparently the doctor didn't even notice them. The grit in the porridge, the dirty pots and pans, the untidy kitchen, the unpleasant odor of the bats, and the unvarying diet obviously were unimportant to him.

One morning I mentioned the grit.

"Gritty? Hmm! I hadn't noticed." Then he asked me to oversee the preparation of the meals. It was a matter of priorities with him. He hadn't time or strength for everything. He chose to do the essentials and paid little attention to the food he ate.

I never met a more faithful man with a greater burden for the souls of the people to whom God had sent him. Every night after supper, we would light a storm lantern and walk to the nearest Fulani camp. There, in the midst of those nomadic cattle-herders, Dr. Stirrett shared the story of God's love, using Hausa, the trade language of the area. Week in and week out this was his life! Nothing else mattered.

Patigi, three miles inland from the Niger River, was the first bridge-head of SIM. Two former attempts to start work in Nigeria had failed. But four young men, Anthony, Banfield, Robinson and Taylor, arriving on the coast in 1901, succeeded the next year in establishing a base there. That autumn, Dr. Stirrett joined them. Then followed difficult years of struggle with disease, the climate, and the powers of darkness. Others came, but the ranks were decimated by death, illness and resignation. When George Sanderson and I arrived, there were only two SIM missionaries in action: Dr. Stirrett at Patigi and Mr. F. E. Hein at Wushishi, farther north.

After I'd been at Patigi about a month, a delegation of believers from Ogga, a Yagba village some 50 miles south, came to see Dr. Stirrett. As Mr. Lang, then on furlough, had suggested the previous Christmas, they'd been praying daily for a missionary. When they'd passed through Patigi market, they'd heard news of a new missionary. As they hurried to see the doctor, their excitement grew. Was the new man the answer to their prayers?

Greetings over, with our visitors comfortably seated on palm frond woven mats, Dr. Stirrett explained to me who they were. They came from Ogga; Mr. Lang had visited them on three occasions. Then the doctor told me the story of how Dani had become a Christian in Lagos, and brought the gospel and a Yoruba Bible back to his village. Dr.

c

Stirrett told me of the growing group of believers there, hungry for teaching and praying for a missionary to go to them. So here I was, face to face with the people I'd heard about in Canada! My heart was moved as I heard their story once again.

"The Yagbas are animists and idol-worshipers. They are bound by fear and superstitions, and they need Jesus," Dr. Stirrett explained.

I went to bed early, but the thought of going so soon into this tribe, not knowing either their language or customs, kept me awake. My mind raced.

About midnight the Lord spoke to me and peace came. Lying there on my bed, in the black stillness, broken only by an occasional birdcall or the high shrilling of a cicada, I recalled Scriptures I'd memorized:

"Fear thou not; for I am with thee: be not dismayed; for I am thy God: I will strengthen thee; yea, I will help thee; yea, I will uphold thee with the right hand of my righteousness. For I the Lord thy God will hold thy right hand, saying unto thee, 'Fear not; I will help thee.'" (Isaiah 41:10, 13)

"Thank you, Lord," I said. Then, with my heart at peace, I slept.

"I'm ready to go," I told the doctor the next morning. We decided it would be better for me to go to Egbe, the largest town in Yagbaland. The men returned to Ogga with this news. At first the group was keenly disappointed, but when reassured that I would visit them frequently, they agreed. To express their joy, they chose a young helper for me, David Adeniyi, named *Osanyigbemi* meaning "the medicine man did well to give me this child."

David, about nine years old, was one of the converts. His father allowed him to come to me on condition that I would teach him more "book." The lad spent about a month with me at Patigi and then we prepared to go to Egbe. It didn't take long to pack; I divided the contents of my trunk into two headloads, and added a bag of salt at Dr. Stirrett's suggestion, to use for barter.

Coins and printed money were unknown among the Yagbas then; cowrie shells were the medium of exchange. Since salt, much desired by the people, was scarce, I could barter for my daily needs.

Now that I was ready, Christians came from Ogga to escort me to Egbe. We started at 5 a.m., walking in single file. At first, the trail led through bush country with tall grass slapping the morning dew on our faces as we passed. Dr. Stirrett accompanied me for a mile or two. Before parting, he committed me to the Lord, handed me two pounds in British money (U.S. $10) and turned back toward Patigi.

I went forward into the unknown, aware of the Lord's presence and claiming His promise, "Fear not; I will help thee."

As we moved away from the Niger River basin, the country changed to thicker underbrush and rolling hills. We didn't see a village, not even a hut, for the first 20 miles. At last, tired and hungry, we arrived at Agboro. Someone must have seen us coming; my arrival caused confusion. The people fled, afraid of my reddish-white skin.

I sought out the chief, visibly frightened himself. However, he gave me a round thatched hut for the night. Hungry? Tired? Yes, but happy! All day long the Lord kept me from danger. At times I'd heard strange sounds, even the roar of unseen animals. Nevertheless, each step of the way God confirmed His promise, "Fear thou not, for I am with thee."

The second day we walked through beautiful wild country, occasionally meeting someone on the trail. We passed few villages, but before dark, came to Odo Okeri. The carriers took me to the chief's compound. I felt so helpless without the language, but they arranged for a hut. When I retired, I lay a long time thinking of home and all that had transpired to bring me to this isolated and perhaps dangerous place. Finally, I drifted off to sleep, unconscious of what was going on outside, but with the Lord's promise reassuring me, "For I the Lord thy God will hold thy right hand, saying unto thee, 'Fear not; I will help thee.'"

We got an early start the next morning as we wanted to arrive at Egbe in good time. As we neared our destination about noon, the bush gave way to farms along the path. I found Egbe a town of considerable size, surrounded by a high mud wall. One entered through high wooden gates which were open during the day and securely locked at night.

As we approached, the watchman, standing above the main gate, leaped to the ground and ran to sound the alarm. Everyone who could run, did, hiding behind huts and trees. Small children, clinging to their mothers, howled in terror. Since the gate was left open, we went on into town to the palace. The chief, wearing a voluminous handwoven blue robe, and bedecked with necklaces of animal claws, leopard teeth, and talismans, gave no evidence of fear, but with great dignity sat on his stool, waiting.

I greeted him in English. He returned the courtesy in Yagba. It didn't matter that neither understood the other. By signs I asked for a place to live. My African helpers further explained my needs, and the chief dispatched a servant to prepare a place for me. The word of the chief was law, and although I didn't know it then, the messenger went to the house chosen and ordered the occupants to leave.

When I was escorted there, I had no intimation of the inconvenience I caused. As I stepped inside the compound wall, I saw small rooms of sun-dried brick with a thatched roof, built in a rectangle around an open courtyard. A pig wallowed contentedly in a mud hole, possibly forgotten in the hasty exit.

My kitchen was a corner of the yard; my stove, three stones, half-buried in the ashes of former fires.

First thing, young David helped me houseclean. We set up my camp cot in one of the rooms. Later, I learned that family graves caused the unevenness of the floor. It was their custom then to bury their dead inside the huts where they'd lived.

Soon the chief sent a pot of water and a bundle of firewood and I prepared a simple meal. The young men who'd carried my loads had already left for Ogga. As night closed in, I felt lonely. Little David and I couldn't converse very well. No one came near. They were afraid.

I wondered how I would communicate the gospel to these people. Being weary after three days on the trail and all the new experiences, I went to bed early. Lying on my cot, I talked things over with my Heavenly Father, who, true to His promise, was with me.

Sleep came slowly as the rhythmic throbbing of drums, the laughter and singing of young people, and the howling of dogs filled my ears. But at last fatigue overcame me, and I slept soundly that first night in Egbe among my people.

4. My fortress

"I will say to the Lord, 'My refuge and my fortress, my God, in whom I trust!'" Psalm 91;2

The people of Egbe were terrified of me. Whenever I showed my face outside the door, everyone fled. If I ventured a few steps from the house in an attempt to make friendly contacts, I could seldom get close enough to speak to anyone. I called, but no one acknowledged my presence; I sang, but seemingly none waited long enough to listen. My presence in the town brought consternation. Only chief Asalu and his retainers allowed me to approach them.

I didn't blame them. Slave raiding was fresh in their memories. All too often strangers had swooped down upon them, carrying off members of their families. Then, too, I learned later of their belief that everything outside of the most ordinary events had to be explained. Therefore, an event such as the coming of a strange-looking creature like me must only result in tragedy.

From the beginning the townspeople called me *Oyinbo*, meaning "man of the peeled skin," for they thought that all were created black but some had the black peeled off.

The bag of salt I'd brought from Patigi proved to be the key. One morning a few days after my arrival, a little lad came wandering by the door of my hut. I reached out and took hold of his hand. Alarmed, he drew back, trying to pull free, but I kept a firm hold and he soon responded to a smile. I put my other hand into a pocket where I'd cached a little salt, and placed a pinch in his hand and a pinch in mine. Touching the salt, I put my finger to my tongue and licked it. The lad did the same and he liked the taste. Whether it was the salt, curiosity, or my smile, I don't know, but the boy became a frequent visitor.

When he brought a few of his buddies, I sang and entertained them to overcome their fear. They carefully examined my clothes and everything I possessed. I couldn't converse with them but I tried to repeat the sounds they made. I pointed to my head and, assuming that they were giving me the word for "head," I'd repeat it and try to remember. Before long I could say a few words—much to their amusement.

Living with the people gave me the greatest chance to learn their language, for I heard men and women talking and children prattling every hour of the day.

Two days before Christmas, I came down with a severe attack of malaria. My body shook from head to toe, and I ached in every joint and muscle. The fever came on all of a sudden. I'd worked hard that morning cleaning up the house, repairing the wall and moving things about. Then about three o'clock malaria struck. Pain spread across my shoulders, down my arms, and my legs lost their strength. My head throbbed; my eyes burned; and I became so cold I couldn't keep my teeth from chattering.

I lay down on my cot and covered myself with all the bedding I had. I was still so cold that I crawled on hands and knees outside the door to lie on the ground in the sun, hoping its warmth would give me a little comfort.

It was my first encounter with malaria. All I knew was to take the powdered quinine that Dr. Stirrett had given me. With David's help, I grasped the bottle. Dipping the spoon into the white powder, I placed the quinine on my tongue. It was terribly bitter. Washing it down with water, I tried to control my nausea as the powder shriveled my mouth and tongue.

As night came, my temperature rose. Occasionally I lapsed into sleep, only to awaken and cry out in pain and misery. Another day and night passed somehow.

Then morning came and as it grew light, I looked around. I was in a strange hut where I must have been carried the night before, to die. The former occupants had left some of their idols and the remnants of sacrifices they'd offered.

I was lying on a sleeping mat spread on the dirt floor. With a pounding headache, and a temperature of over 103, I realized it was Christmas morning.

David came near and asked, "Oyinbo, should I go for help?"

Dr. Stirrett lived in Patigi. "No, I could be dead before the doctor arrived."

"What shall I do?"

"We will ask the Lord Jesus to heal me, if He will."

The lad opened his eyes wide. With a stammering tongue, I told him Jesus was right here with us and that He would help. He knelt down beside me. I was too weak to rise, so lying there on the floor, I lifted up my heart to God, praying that He would undertake for me and restore my health.

In the throes of more chills, I had David pile on the bedding and I took another dose of quinine. Some time later I began to perspire. The fever broke, and my temperature lowered rapidly. Sick, weak, and isolated, I spent my first Christmas in Africa. I went back to my hut.

Later, David brought food. As I looked at the palm oil dinner, I thought of the turkey dinners at home, but I took a taste so David wouldn't feel bad.

That day the chief had called the men home from their farms to repair the wall around the town. As was the custom, drummers and horn-blowers played as they worked.

Next door to me a man lay dying of sleeping sickness. My head throbbed as I had to listen to hopeless wailing of his wives and the deafening noise of the music.

Most of all, I longed for companionship. Here I was, a 27-year-old bachelor, alone, but not by choice.

The next day I slept late, but wakened to hear footsteps approaching

outside. There was Mr. Lang from Patigi, stooping to enter the low
doorway. I tried to rise, but fell back upon my cot; then I cried like a
baby. God had sent my fellow-missionary, the first one I'd seen since
coming to Egbe.

Mr. Lang knelt beside me, and putting his hand on my forehead said,
"Why, brother Titcombe, you have a fever!"

I told him I'd been ill for three days. What a difference it made just
to have him there with me! I looked into his face and thanked God. I
thought of those at home who'd never been far from family and accustomed scenes, who didn't fully appreciate the privilege and joy of
Christian fellowship. Although news of my illness hadn't reached
Patigi, God knew, and put it in Mr. Lang's heart to come and visit
me for a few days.

I enjoyed being with another missionary and talking in English
again. But eventually I fell asleep from sheer weariness.

As the days and weeks passed and I learned a little more of the
language, I began to move around among the people of the town. They,
in turn, overcame their fear of my white face and strange appearance.

I observed how completely the worship of their many gods and the
subjugation of all other concerns to the appeasement of the spirit world
controlled the Yagba way of life.

They, like the Yorubas, of which they are a sub-tribe, were animists.
Near the doorway of each household they placed a mound of earth on
the one side and a large stone on the other. The one represented *Olorun*
and the other *Esu*. They offered sacrifices of animals and fowl to these
gods. The area would be strewn with feathers and bones, and stained
with blood. Like animistic people throughout the world, they had some
knowledge of a Supreme Being. The Yoruba called Him Olorun, the
"Owner of Heaven," for whom they had reverential fear. He was a long
way off, and as far as they knew paid little attention to them, so they
reciprocated in kind. Esu, the god of all evil, on the other hand, seemed
near and his power real.

Ignorance and fear, due to a lack of understanding of the scientific
explanation of natural phenomena, dominated their religious life.
They feared what they didn't understand, and they believed that
nature was cruel and demanding. They hoped that by showing fear
and respect for the unknown powers, they would gain favor and possibly
avoid the evil consequences of displeasing them.

Each large house or cluster of huts had carved wooden idols, many
of them grotesque, housed in a small shelter, and worshiped by the

local people. Witch doctors and priestesses devoted their days to sacrificial rites. They served as intermediaries between the people and the gods whom the idols represented.

I found that their social and religious life was not as disorganized as I'd thought. Irrevocable rules governed their manner of life. To them, every unusual happening must be explained. Severe tropical storms occurred during the wet season. The rumbling thunder and fearful lightning terrified them. They believed these demonstrated the thunder god's anger, so they made a god to represent him, calling him *Shango*. When lightning struck a house, the priest devoted to Shango hurried there and forbade anyone entering. Poking about in the rubble, he would produce the "thunderbolt" which had caused the damage. This was, no doubt, something he'd brought concealed on his person, but because of the fear of the people, served as a reasonable explanation. The priest announced to the assembled crowd that Shango was angry and had given vent to his ire by sending the thunderbolt. He demanded a substantial sacrifice from the unfortunate household, collected anything of value left after the fire, and made off with his booty.

The Yagbas suffered much from the caprices of *Osain*, god of sickness and health. With no understanding of the germ theory, antisepsis, and the science of medicine, they needed help to combat this powerful enemy. So when illness came, they sought the medicine man's help. His knowledge was a combination of folklore, superstition, true knowledge of the efficacy of some herbs, and mumbo-jumbo, all mixed together to give him uncontested power over the people. He explained that the sick person had offended the god Osain and must therefore appease him. He would demand a chicken, goat or other valuable possession in order to perform the rites and offer a sacrifice to appease the offended god's anger.

Unfortunately, this also worked another way. A person could pay the medicine man to bring a curse upon an enemy or even destroy a life.

The Yagbas, like people everywhere, sought to know the future. They wouldn't take a wife, erect a house, plant or harvest crops, without first showing some recognition of the spirits and gods who governed their lives. The priest appointed for this purpose used various methods. Answers came in the entrails of fowls or animals sacrificed; the omens of the heavenly bodies; or the arrangement of curiously colored and shaped stones when cast on the ground. These supposedly served to give foreknowledge and advice concerning the future.

The Yagbas practiced *Egungun*, the worship of ancestors.

Ogun, the god of war and anything made of iron was the patron of all blacksmiths and soldiers, who sacrificed faithfully to him.

The people practiced fertility rites. Women continually sought the favor of *Igunnu*, the god of motherhood. Childless wives were believed to have incurred his disfavor. Such unfortunate women were cruelly tormented, and life for them was one continual round of sacrifices and of seeking from Igunnu the divine favor of childbearing. When the offerings and sacrifices made through the help of a priest or priestess of Igunnu in one place proved unsuccessful, they made long journeys to seek the help and blessing of other mediators, in the vain hope that they would become mothers.

The Yagbas believed that the spirit world, though unseen, was real and continually surrounded them. They sought the blessing of the spirit world in every activity, and to offend, whether through neglect or by conscious act, was unthinkable.

So I found that the Yagbas lived in constant fear, and spent their days in a continual round of sacrifices and superstition in the hope that evil would be averted and good fortune come their way.

5. He delivers

"For it is He who delivers you from the snare of the trapper, and from the deadly pestilence." Psalm 91:3

I worked hard at learning the language, using David as my informant. In fact, we spent so much time studying together that David's duties in the kitchen were sadly neglected.

The visits I made to Ogga also helped me with the language. The believers there wanted teaching so badly that I was simply forced into learning as fast as I could.

I was encouraged every time I went to them. They showed me the church they had just built, and when I stepped inside I could have wept for joy. I wished the people at home could have seen it. They would never ask again if it had been worth the sacrifice and money to go and tell them of Jesus. A sight like that was better than the riches of the world, and it encouraged me to work and pray more.

After about six months I gave my first public message in the Yagba language. I preached in the market place of Egbe. It was a feeble effort, but an exciting beginning.

But as soon as I returned to my hut, chief Asalu sent for me. Going at once, I found him in an angry mood. He warned that if I wanted to speak to his people, I'd do it before him.

Seeking to mollify him, I said, "All right, chief, I'm ready."

He gathered 12 of his retainers about him and I haltingly gave them the gospel. I thanked the chief for the privilege and then added, "It's not only to you and the old men that I've come. I want to speak to the whole Yagba tribe."

Up until then, neither the chief nor the witch doctor had shown any opposition. I thought the chief my friend, although he didn't understand my real purpose. However, as I heard more of the language, I realized his friendliness was superficial. He was actually fearful and jealous. The people gave him gifts for me; some he passed on, others he kept for himself.

One morning I awoke to find a powder on my pillow. I chided David for not shaking the dust from my pillow when he tucked in the mosquito net the night before. When he examined the powder, his eyes grew big with fright.

"That's poison," he said. "The witch doctor concocted it and had someone put it there, hoping that you would inhale it and die."

The wicked old man realized that if the people accepted the gospel, he would lose his power to deceive them, so he plotted to destroy me.

Only those who have lived in an animistic culture can fully understand the feeling of oppression and satanic power. It is enough to shake anyone to the depths of his being; the "rulers of the darkness of this world" were rallying against me. Satan knew that my presence in Egbe as a representative of Jesus Christ challenged his power. He sought my destruction.

I refused to be intimidated. God was with me, and nothing can compare to the thrill of being thrust completely on Him and to see divine deliverance come!

A few days later, young David brought me a small piece of raw cotton. Opening it I found a sharp, poison-tipped thorn. "Where did you find this, David?"

"On the floor beside your bed."

It had been put there during the night with the hope that when I got up I would step on it and die. My heart cried out, "Thank you, Lord, for watching over me. Your Word is true. You will not allow my foot to slip; you will not slumber."

Opposition continued from more official sources, but I was not deterred. The chief sent a slave to follow me as I visited the surrounding villages. When I'd move on, this man would stay behind to counteract all I'd said. I could only be faithful and commit my cause to God.

When chief Asalu found that the witch doctor's poison didn't get rid of me, he sent to another tribe and invited a Muslim teacher to come to Egbe to perform his prayers outside my hut. Five times a day for three months this man persisted, without apparent effect. Then, discouraged, he complained to the chief, "It's no use. His God is stronger than mine."

The battle continued. It would not be easy to break the bands of superstition and the evil practices binding the people; yet eventually, with God's help, I knew we would win.

The first real break came unexpectedly. One day while I was studying Yagba with David, a young fellow about 12 years old came near. After greetings, I asked what he wanted. He got down on his knees and said, "I want to be your boy."

I asked who his father was. "He's the witch doctor of my town, but he won't care."

When I enquired what kind of work he could do, he said he'd do anything. With David to supervise, I gladly turned the kitchen over to him. I showed him how to make biscuits, using palm oil instead of shortening, baking them in an oven made of an earthenware pot placed on a crude stand over my stove of three stones.

I didn't ask questions, and it worked out fine. Life was simple: breakfast after dawn, lunch about noontime, and the evening meal at dusk. We didn't need a clock or watch. What mattered was that I'd come to spend my life here, and having Aliyu cook gave me more time to study the language.

Aliyu, however, was given to petty theft. This really upset me.

One day he came to me and asked, "Oyinbo, why are you weeping? Is it because I stole sugar?"

I replied, "No, not really. The sugar itself isn't important. It's because I thought you were my friend. I trusted you, but now I see that you are not really my friend."

Two weeks later Aliyu accepted Christ as his Savior. Knowing that his father, the witch doctor, made poison for the people of that area, I was amazed to think that a boy coming from such a home had become my first convert.

Aliyu stood firm, and became an important witness. When he became a young man and his father became seriously ill, Aliyu went home and sat beside him telling him of the Savior. We couldn't be sure, but we hope that the old man believed before he died. The father left eleven wives. According to tribal custom, the boy inherited them. What would he do?

At his father's graveside, Aliyu turned to these women and said, "I am a believer in Jesus. You are not on the same road that I am following, so I dismiss you all. You may go, but I want your children to stay so that I can teach them the words of Jesus."

The young lad's action caused a great uproar in the village. Such a thing had never been done before; his association with the white man; his forsaking the witchcraft of his father; his refusing to inherit his father's wives caused a tense situation.

The chief called Aliyu, but cajoling and threats didn't change his mind. He was sent to Patigi to be judged by a Muslim judge. This man, with the consent of the British official, put Aliyu into prison.

The old chief boasted, "Now we'll never be bothered with that fellow again!"

However, his victory was short-lived. In Patigi one night the white official was awakened from sleep to see someone standing beside him. He called out, "Who is it? What do you want?"

"What about the boy in prison?" a voice asked.

The next morning, a shaken government official went to the prison and spoke to Aliyu personally. Hearing his story, the man told the judge that Aliyu should be released. The boy refused to go. Puzzled, the official asked why.

"Take me to my town," Aliyu said. "I'm innocent. I'm here because I'm a Christian. I didn't do the things I've been accused of."

The British official realized that some sort of chicanery was responsible for the boy's apprehension, and was kind enough to escort him home.

6. Under His wings

"He will cover you with His pinions, and under His wings you may seek refuge." Psalm 91:4

In less than a year after I reached Egbe, I saw the church of Jesus Christ established in Yagbaland.

I had visited the believers at Ogga frequently, and by October of 1909 the first group was ready for baptism. Earlier in the year they had built their church building, and I had gone to dedicate it. The building was 24 feet long, with rows of mud seats on either side of a central aisle. At the front they'd built a pulpit with steps up to it and a circular seat behind it for the preacher. When I dedicated it, I wished brother Lang might have had the privilege, for it was he who first trekked into

Yagbaland in 1905 and discovered Dani and the handful of believers there at Ogga.

I left Egbe early in October to spend several weeks with them. Imagine my joy, after walking 18 miles from Egbe on a trail that climbed over a high pass and brought me down to the bank of the Campee River, to see a good company of young men waiting to help me across. Entering the town, I found a large group waiting outside Dani's compound.

I held a service each afternoon, but person-to-person talks accomplished more. At the first meeting I invited any who wished, to come to my room. Almost every morning some of the lads gathered for three hours at a time asking questions about the Bible. I was surprised how easily they turned up the chapter and verse as I referred to portions of the Bible.

I realized how profitable it was that I spoke Yoruba so they could talk to me directly. They felt free to share things they would not discuss through an interpreter. They were so hungry for the Word that as I sat outside after my supper, they'd gather to hear more. But, praise God, they had the Bible in their language, so the Holy Spirit could teach them whether I was there or not. During those days I tried to show them their responsibility to go to other villages with the gospel.

Every evening I taught them hymns and often they'd keep me going until eleven o'clock. But oh, what a joy it was to be with them! I don't know what the Lord saw in me to choose me for this work, for I am not worthy of such a privilege.

Each morning the young men rose early, met to sing a hymn, prayed, then left for their farms so they could be back for an afternoon service. As I lay in bed and heard them singing praises to their Savior, my heart was full of joy. I was greatly impressed one morning as they sang, "Holy, Holy, Holy, Lord God Almighty." Five years before, Dani had returned to Ogga to tell his people about Jesus. Now about forty met morning after morning to praise and worship God together. Who had accomplished this miracle? Not man, but God. I was inspired as I realized He'd helped me in the past, He would in the future; what He did at Ogga, He would do at Egbe and other places if we were faithful.

A large group of young believers there needed wives. Only one was married so we prayed that more young women would believe so they could become their wives.

I asked the Lord to so immerse me in His love that I could lead them on to know Him better.

For some time these young people had talked of being baptized. Now I felt some were ready, so I sent messengers to Dr. Stirrett and my newly-arrived co-worker, Fred Rutherford, to come and help me establish the first young church in Yagbaland.

Dr. Stirrett and Fred arrived Saturday, October 30. At seven the next morning we all left for the river. What a sight! Sixty-eight people walked single file, singing their favorite hymn, "I Will Follow Jesus Anywhere." After an hour we arrived; the candidates wore white, and the scene beside the stream was most impressive.

The doctor spoke, and then baptized 13—ten men and three women. I wish you could have seen their faces, illuminated with the joy and happiness that Jesus gives.

That night, Fred Rutherford preached to a packed church. Afterwards, the 16 of us sat down to the Lord's Supper and He made himself very real. This was a milestone. Sixteen years had passed since our first pioneers, Bingham, Gowans and Kent, had ventured by faith into the interior of Nigeria. Within six months two of them died. Now here was the promised fruit. The young church was born!

When I went back to Egbe, I had Fred Rutherford as my companion. He had been appointed to work with me at Egbe, and after nearly a year of being entirely on my own, it was joy unspeakable to have a white companion.

The last day of the year I returned to Ogga for another "first," a watchnight service. To show their joy, the believers made palm branch arches before the church door and at the entrance of the house where I stayed.

Then the next morning, New Year's Day 1910, after I'd spoken, we opened the meeting for testimonies. As I heard how God had blessed them, some saying this was their first New Year with Jesus, I wept for joy. A dear sister said, "I have suffered a great deal in body this past year. I cannot understand why, but the Lord knows what is best for me."

Then they brought gifts to the Lord and put them in an old straw hat. The money amounted to 13 shillings (about $3.50). In many cases, they gave all they had. Why? Because since Jesus had loved them enough to give His life for them, they wanted to show their love for Him in return.

On this New Year's Day I claimed Jeremiah 33:3, "Call unto me, and I will answer thee, and shew thee great and mighty things, which thou knowest not" for Egbe and Yagbaland. The Lord made good this promise immediately.

D

7. Not afraid

"You will not be afraid of the terror by night, or of the arrow that flies by day." Psalm 91:5

In the early days the people didn't understand why I'd come, and they kept their distance. Chief Asalu and some of the headmen intensified this misunderstanding by using me to further their own schemes. They told the people not to visit us.

By January 1910, Fred, my co-worker, and I decided that if the chief wouldn't allow the people to come to us, we would go to the people. Night after night we went to Ilegbemi's compound. He was a young believer who wasn't afraid to have us. As I preached, Fred and the

Christians prayed. The people welcomed us and grew bold enough to come and visit us. This enraged the chief, who realized that as his people turned from idols to God, he would lose his share of the revenue from all the sacrifices made.

"It's all right to preach to me and my sub-chiefs, but leave the lower classes alone," he ordered.

What should we do? We prayed, and decided to be true to our commission. This resulted in our first breach with chief Asalu. Now he began to show his true character. Previously, he had, without our knowledge, used us as a threat to force his people's obedience.

This crisis proved the truth of Romans 8:28! The common people now realized that we were not "the chief's white men," as he had led them to believe, but that we'd come to be their friends and to share the gospel with them, too.

Until late 1909 the congregation in our daily service had averaged about ten. However, as I gained facility in speaking Yagba and visited the people in their homes, they began to realize that I was one with them. Now, immediately after I'd claimed the promise of Jeremiah 33:3 on New Year's Day, we counted about 200 adults at our daily services. Several nights over 40 women came. As soon as we rang the bell, people began coming from all directions. My heart was blessed to hear them learning to sing hymns. They would listen eagerly to the message, drinking in every word. After I finished, our laborer would add a word, and then we all knelt in prayer. A few became Christians.

One night, Igbemani, a recent convert, stood and said to the people, "You all know me. You know I used to kill dogs, chickens, goats and pigs for the idols."

"Yes."

Then he told them how he had destroyed his idols and was now following Jesus. He told them Jesus satisfied him every day, and that when he went to his farm, He went with him and helped him.

Soon after this, one of the young converts was severely tested. The chief called for him, and taking him to the idol house demanded, "Sayomi, make an offering to this idol!"

Bowing respectfully to the chief, Sayomi replied, "O King, I can no longer worship this idol. Jesus has made my stomach sweet."

When Sayomi still refused even after severe threats, he was tied securely hand and foot and beaten until his back was lacerated and raw, then left outside in the hot sun. He crawled to my house and I cared for him.

God was calling out a people for His name. Soon 11 young men had witnessed their faith in Jesus Christ. When the witch doctor tried to poison them, they moved in with me. The idol worshipers joined the witch doctor and marched and danced around my house, singing and shouting profanity and demonstrating their hatred toward their brothers. The chief forbade anyone from bringing food to us. It was not safe to leave the house.

I was unprepared for this outbreak of persecution; nevertheless, God knew. A man had come to me a day or so before, to borrow money to pay his taxes. He'd brought a basket of corn for security. From the start I'd decided never to lend money, so I purchased the corn. This was our only food, so we had it day after day.

After a week of this coarse diet, I awakened one morning with severe cramps and soon discovered I had dysentery. The very smell of the corn cooking nauseated me.

"I can't eat any more corn. I'm sick."

"I'll go out and get you something else to eat," Ilegbemi said.

"No! If you go out of that door, you'll die."

"No matter," he replied, "if I don't go, you'll die. Then what will we do?"

"Never mind if I die. God will not die. He is greater than a missionary. But let's pray about it."

We knelt on the ground together to pray. I was weak and sick yet deeply touched by the concern of these young believers. All I could say was the Lord's Prayer: "Our Father, which art in heaven, Hallowed be thy name. Thy kingdom come. Thy will be done in earth, as it is in heaven. Give us *this* day our daily bread. . ."

I got no further. "Thank you, Lord," I broke down and wept. My companions were as quiet as death. After a few moments of silence, I stood up, puzzled. How could we get other food, surrounded as we were by the chief, witch doctor, and angry villagers?

The day passed slowly. I was ill and uncomfortable. We encouraged one another by remembering that God was still on His throne. He was alive and cared for us.

Evening came and when the others had eaten some corn, they soon fell asleep. Later, I heard someone at the door call, "Oyinbo!"

The believers woke and called to me, "Don't open the door, don't open the door, Oyinbo!"

I told them to take the bar from the door. They did. Fearfully they drew the flimsy door open. There stood one of the chief's underlings, accompanied by another man.

"What do you want?" I asked.

"Oyinbo, the chief has ordered that you are all to be killed. I have brought my slave. He will fight for you."

"Thank you, but I do not need your slave."

"But, Oyinbo, you don't have a gun or sword."

"True, I don't, but I have the living God. My help comes from the Lord, who made heaven and earth. He who keeps me will not slumber or sleep."

The man turned and whispered to his slave, who reached into a basket and pulled out a duck. He laid it at my feet, and then they left.

I remembered. That morning we'd prayed, "Give us *this* day our daily bread." God answered prayer before the day ended. The men didn't even wait to pluck the feathers; they singed them off, and soon the duck was in the pot cooking.

A few days later, we heard singing and shouting from a hilltop on the far side of town. Peering out, one of my companions said, "Oyinbo, they're all up on the hill." Unbarring the door, we stepped out into the village. It was great to be in the open again. The fellows scattered in search of food. They hadn't gone far when the group on the hill rushed down toward us, brandishing clubs and knives.

I felt weak, but as I sat watching them come, I knew the Lord Jesus would undertake. The boys begged me to go back into the hut. "No, you go back, I'm going to stay right here."

The crowd came nearer and nearer. The 11 young men, concerned for my safety, formed a ring around me. If anyone was going to get hurt, they determined it would be them first. God had truly knit our hearts together in love for each other.

The animists, running and jumping, shouting and screaming, came on, but when they reached about 50 feet from me, they stumbled and fell, piling up on one another. That took the fire out of them. They got to their feet, looking somewhat sheepish.

"Why did you stop? Why didn't you attack me?" I asked them.

"We couldn't. Someone held us back."

"Why?" God did it. I clearly recall my thoughts at that moment. My Lord in His great commission reassured me, "I am with you always."

During the days and nights we'd been trapped in the hut with the townspeople singing and dancing hour after hour, their songs had be-

come firmly fixed in my mind. Now I got up and walked slowly toward them. Using one of their tunes I began to sing:
Thank you very much, Jesus came into the world for me.
Thank you very much, He suffered for me.
Thank you very much, He died for me.
As the words continued to come, I shared the gospel. It wasn't long before the crowd began to sway to the rhythm. One by one they dropped their weapons and sat down.

Among them was Daeke, the witch doctor. He'd tried to poison me and had done everything he could to turn the people against me and the gospel.

"I've tried to help your sick ones and those in trouble," I said. "I've never taken anything from you unless I paid for it." I pointed to Daeke. "There is Daeke," I said. "He takes your food, your chickens, your money, and deceives you over and over. Why do you listen to him? I have come to tell you of Jesus, who died for you, who lives, and who is able to save you from your sins."

The people sat and listened intently for about two hours. The Spirit of God moved among them in convicting power.

Some time later I learned that while we were going through this ordeal, a company of people in my home church in Hamilton, Canada, was praying. It was while they prayed that God delivered us. That was a turning point. In the months that followed, the Holy Spirit brought hundreds to Christ.

As more and more took their stand for Christ, the company of believers grew bolder. Several brought their idols to destroy them, knowing their actions would bring much opposition. When those who believed stood firm, others gained courage to do the same, until there were more than 50 professing Christians. To be sure, they didn't understand all the gospel meant, yet with honest hearts before God and man, they desired a true knowledge of Him.

We can only estimate the number of idols destroyed, but we know of at least 200. Two places of idol worship in Ainke, the section of Egbe where I'd recently built a house and moved from the original borrowed house I first stayed in, were knocked down. So much was going on every day.

At the beginning, I simply stood in the open or under a shade tree; crowds gathered and I preached to them. Before there were any believers, a friend in Hamilton had sent $50 and I had put up a small "church" 18 feet by 20 feet. This soon became too small. Praise the

Lord, it was the only church built with help from outside. As soon as men believed, they built their own churches.

Now the believers took a great step forward when they built their own place of worship, a mud-walled, grass-roofed building 36 feet by 60 feet. They didn't need a plan, as they knew only one way to build. They simply made the church like their homes, only larger. There was no need of a campaign to raise funds. It was their church, so they worked with willing hands and joyful hearts. And there was no doubt that as these loving souls and their missionaries gathered there, God met with us to bless.

I am so grateful that God gave me wisdom in establishing right methods and relationships from the beginning. It would have been easier, perhaps quicker, to have interfered in the development of the church by introducing Western ways. God helped me wait and pray. As long as they depended on me, they would remain weak. So as they learned to look to God directly, they became strong.

Trouble flared up again. When the Christians cleared the piece of land to build their church, they cut down part of a grove of trees. This angered the chief and townspeople. The Yagbas at that time were under the Nupes, with headquarters at Patigi; so the chief sent a delegation to the British Resident at Patigi with many false accusations. I followed.

"What's going on at Egbe anyway, Mr. Titcombe?" the Resident asked me.

I told him. When he learned that the matter concerned a few trees, not belonging to anyone in particular, he said, "Well, is that all? The accusations brought to me by the chief's men sounded as though the whole town was at everyone's throat."

As a result, the Resident went to Ere, a town part way to Egbe, called chief Asalu to meet him there, and because of his evil practices through the years, banished him and his wives to Okeloke, where he died.

Soon I began to see the fruit of the Spirit in lives. Here were erstwhile animists, now completely turned around. In Egbe town in the morning, the first one awake would start a song, and the refrain would be taken up all over town as believers got up and prepared for the day. Their favorite was a loose translation of "There Is a Fountain Filled with Blood." As the singing ended, family groups prayed together before going to their farms. They lived in Egbe and went out to their farms in the surrounding countryside. Those whose farms were more distant would remain on them Monday through Friday, then come in for the weekend. They learned quickly that Sunday was the Lord's Day and spent it in worship rather than work. They gladly accepted this pattern, even though at this time they couldn't read and so didn't own their own Bibles.

Returning from their farms for the weekend, they'd stop at the pool on the edge of town to wash their clothes. Then they'd spread them out on the grass and bushes and wait for them to dry. Up until now, only locally woven clothes made by sewing narrow strips together were available. Now the young men wanted to wear clothes like ours. Itinerant traders soon learned of this new market and began to bring imported cloth from the coast. I observed that they were exploiting the Christians unmercifully by overcharging them.

"You'd better reduce your prices or I'll lick you at your own game," I told the traders one day. They laughed at me. Although I didn't have much money, I used what I had and sent four boys to Ilorin to buy cloth. I wrote a note to the trader there explaining my purpose, and he filled my order at a reasonable price. Within two days, the cloth was all sold, at half the price the traders had charged, and I still received 100 percent profit. Then I stocked a small store with some of the most needful articles for the people, and I used all the profits to buy medicines for the dispensary.

Fred Rutherford and I really enjoyed our simple but comfortable new house. It was in town, close to the people, but a place of our own. The new chief, Agbana, frequently visited me, and as soon as the church was finished he came to every service and sat with his people, listening to the words of God.

Previously, the people were afraid of chief Asalu. Now, with chief Agbana attending, they had nothing to fear. Weekday meetings averaged 400; Sunday mornings, Fred and I spoke six or eight times, I to a packed church, and he to overflow crowds outside. The Sunday afternoon service now averaged 1200, made up of about 35 percent men, 40 percent women and the rest children, mostly between the ages of 10 and 15.

The growing medical work, care of the new converts, language study for both Fred and me, reading classes, preaching and teaching, packed our days full. Then we had visitors constantly; chief Agbana came almost daily. We were thrilled with all that God was doing!

Now that Fred shared the Egbe responsibilities with me, I determined to trek to the villages.

8. Destruction at noon

"Of the pestilence that stalks in darkness, or of the destruction that lays waste at noon." Psalm 91:6

Boom! Ba-ba-boom! Boom! Ba-ba-boom! Drums telegraphed news to the next village, "Oyinbo Egbe is coming." With Fred at Egbe, I was free to trek to the villages. David of Ogga, my right-hand man, helped me prepare headloads with the essentials: camp cot and mosquito net, food and cooking utensils, a folding chair and table, and a kerosene lamp.

One day we reached the town of Isanlu to find it was market day. I took advantage of a great crowd of people in the market place and began to preach to them. I noticed they were restless and wondered why.

Then I heard drums and horns. The crowd fell back, trampling one another, with their eyes fastened on something behind me. I turned to see the chief, surrounded by his retainers, approaching, obviously angry. It was a frightening sight; he appeared to be drunk. The deafening sound, together with the frenzied dancing of his slaves brandishing swords and bows and arrows, would have put fear in anyone. Reaching the open area where I stood, they spread a leopard's skin on the ground and the chief sat down on it.

I approached him to pay my respects. "Oh, King, I'm glad to see you today. I've come to tell you and your people of the true and living God."

While I spoke, the chief staggered to his feet, and snatching a sword from one of his men, began waving it back and forth before the crowd.

"If anyone accepts this Oyinbo's teaching . . ." he drew the sword across his throat. Then he turned on me.

With the sword inches above my head, I remembered Psalm 91:1: "He that dwelleth in the secret place of the most High shall abide under the shadow of the Almighty."

"Oh, King," I said, "I am dwelling . . . in the shadow of the Almighty God!"

The sword dropped; the chief bellowed like an angry bull; the people fled, leaving my companions and me alone in the market place. Even though I was only five feet three inches tall and unarmed, I knew God wouldn't fail me. He promised I would "tread upon the lion!"

A few days later, my carriers and I approached Kponyan. I'd heard incredible stories about this place. As we followed the trail through dense jungle, we came upon three skulls slung on a vine across the path, barring entrance to the village.

When my companions saw that, they dropped the "chop" box, and the other head-loads and kneeling at my feet declared emphatically, "Oyinbo, we can't go any farther!"

"Why? I am. I must go!"

They were terrified. I prayed, but they still refused to go on. So I told them to go back down the trail and wait. "Keep the skulls in view; wait until the sun sets. If I don't come back by then, take your loads and run for home."

They begged me not to pass. The fear in their faces spoke as eloquently as their trembling voices. But I felt the Lord would have me go on. I waited until they had gone back a piece, and set their loads down.

Then, praying and whispering the name of Jesus, I got down on my hands and knees and slowly crawled under the skulls. One of them touched my back. It scared me but I kept on going. About 50 feet ahead there was a large shade tree; I sat down, and leaned against it, tired and thirsty.

Presently, a girl with a waterpot on her head approached. She didn't notice me. I called, asking for a drink. She froze in her tracks. Obviously confused, she evidently didn't want to give me water, but was too afraid to refuse. When I'd had a drink, she picked up her pot and fled into the village.

I walked toward the town. Passing through the gate, I proceeded to the chief's compound. Pausing at the door of his entrance hut, I noticed numerous other skulls hanging from the rafters.

The chief emerged, evidently furious. He stalked back and forth shouting at the top of his voice that I was the son of a monkey, a dog, a pig, and other things, none of which I appreciated.

"Lord, I don't know what I've done to incur this, but please help me out of this jam," I prayed.

I learned that the chief was angry because I'd spoken to a woman before greeting him. Then God answered my hurried, informal prayer. A woman appeared, carrying a calabash of food on her head. Kneeling before the chief, she placed it on the mat at his feet. This diverted his attention, and he stopped raving at me.

Among the Yagba people, courtesy demands that anybody near must be invited to eat with you. Another man standing nearby was invited to join the chief. They sat down and soon began putting their fingers in the food.

"Wait a minute. Aren't you the chief?" I asked.

He looked up indignantly and striking his chest with his fist, exclaimed, "Certainly, I'm chief of this whole territory."

"I can hardly believe it," I said, "for you are eating food and yet you are treating me in a way your lowest subject wouldn't."

"What do you mean?"

"Here I am, a stranger who has come to your door; you are eating with your friend, but you haven't asked me to eat with you."

"Would you eat with me?"

"You haven't asked me."

Then he invited me to join them. I looked at the food. The gravy didn't look like anything I'd eaten before. Then I thought of what Paul said in I Corinthians 9:22: "I am made all things to all men, that I might by all means save some."

I sat down with them and said: "I never eat anything until I ask God's blessing on the food He has given."

They watched me suspiciously. They'd never seen anyone bow his head in prayer before.

The blessing asked, I put my hand in, picked up a portion, put it in my mouth and let it slide down. It was hot with pepper and burned all the way to my stomach. I ate a second portion. They watched me carefully.

Then suddenly the old chief jumped to his feet and said, with a big smile, "Oyinbo, you are my friend forever!"

"If I'm your friend," I said, "what about my three young men outside the village?"

"Call them, Oyinbo. You are my friend, and that includes those with you."

I got up and returned along the path to call the carriers. When they heard my voice, they came running. They were too afraid to crawl under the skulls, but pushed their way through the heavy undergrowth beside the path. I took them to the chief's compound, where he and his friend were still sitting beside the calabash. The boys ate the food the chief offered and then they made me a cup of tea to help settle my stomach. I offered some to the chief, but he refused.

After a while I asked him to call his people as I had something to tell them. He gathered a few old men. I urged him to call all the townspeople, the women and children as well as the men.

"We are the people," he said, "the women are only animals."

Then I began to sing the gospel using their familiar tunes. Soon everyone, including women and children, gathered around. Since they knew the tunes and I repeated the words over and over, they began to sing with me, slowly swaying from side to side.

Then I'd give them a short message and we'd sing some more. This continued for more than an hour; but being tired from all the excitement, I suggested we rest. The chief invited me to use his hut. I declined, preferring to sleep out under the trees.

As I lay, half awake and half asleep, I could hear the old men discussing the things I'd said.

"This Oyinbo speaks of a strange God who loves people. Whoever heard of a God like that? We don't know of a God of love, only a God of anger."

The next day I visited from door to door, inviting everyone to come to the chief's compound that evening, as I had more to tell them. Several hundred came. The same thing happened the next night. After several days I told the chief I would be leaving the next morning. He begged me to stay, as he wanted to hear more.

The mosquitoes were so bad that night that the chief commanded that a smudge fire be kindled. This helped a little. Then for several hours I went over the gospel story again and again.

During the night, a young man came secretly, asking if God knew all things. Did He know about the blood on his hands? I told him that indeed God certainly knew if there was blood on his hands, and more than that, He knew all the sin of his heart. Then I told him that the blood of Jesus Christ, shed on Calvary's cross, could cleanse his heart and make it "cleaner than the white clouds in the sky."

"My heart?"

"Yes, your heart."

At dawn I went to say goodbye to the chief. He and others accompanied us along the trail as an act of courtesy. When he reached the string of skulls, the chief himself untied the vine, drew it aside, and we walked by.

Then the chief knelt at my feet, looked up into my face and asked, "You will come back again, Oyinbo?"

"Yes, I will come again."

Two years passed before I returned to Kponyan. As I approached the village, I noticed the string of skulls was gone.

Seeing a man sitting on a mat and leaning against the wall I asked, "Where is my old friend, the chief?"

"He is dead. We have been looking down the trail for many moons, watching for you. You promised to return."

As I enquired further, I was told that when the old chief lay dying he kept saying over and over, "Jesu, Jesu."

I believe that one day I am going to see the chief in glory.

For a long time I'd wanted to visit Mopa. Walking there one day I enjoyed the beauty of the hills and valleys in their green jungle finery. Africa, and especially this part where the Yagbas lived, was entrancing and exciting. My heart was full and my voice filled the forest with singing as my friends and I walked single file along the path. So I was completely unprepared for the surprising experiences ahead.

We entered the town and went to the chief's compound. No one appeared. This was unusual; I could hear voices, but didn't see anyone.

Usually, when a stranger arrives, lodging and wood and water are provided. But though I waited some time, no one came. I asked my carriers what I should do. They decided to go in search of wood and water themselves.

I walked to the top of a nearby hill. There I sang and preached to the village. Although I couldn't see anyone, I knew people could hear me. I was determined to share the gospel with them.

That night we slept out under a tree. The next day I preached again from the hilltop. Still no one appeared.

The third night as I was retiring, my companions said, "Will you leave your lantern burning tonight?"

"Why?"

"Well, we wish you would."

I did. I noticed that night the boys lay close beside me.

Before I fell asleep, I heard a voice out of the darkness, "Oyinbo."

"Who's there?" I asked, jumping out of bed.

A young man came into the circle of light, and falling to his knees said, "Oyinbo, I've been listening as you sang and talked from the hilltop. You said that someone died for me. Tell me more."

I sat on the edge of my camp cot and explained to him how Christ died on the cross for his sins. What a joy it was, after talking with him for an hour or so, to introduce him to Jesus Christ.

After we'd prayed together, I said, "Son, why is it that I've been here three days and I haven't seen anyone? I know there are people here, for I've heard voices."

The young man leaned forward and whispered, "Oyinbo, there is a thing going on in the village. See that hut over there? It's an idol house. A sacrifice was made there—a young girl. All the villagers have fled to the forest. Only the witch doctors and chief men are in town."

He took us to the hut and drew aside the mat at the doorway. In the flickering light of the lantern we saw the evidences of that ritual. Appalled, we broke camp immediately and left, even though it was the middle of the night. After walking five or six miles along the trail with only the night sounds of birds and shrilling cicadas for company, we waited for the morning under some trees.

I couldn't sleep as I thought how deep was the darkness, not only of the tropical night around us, but of the hearts of these people bound by Satan. How I longed to tell them of Jesus Christ, who could break their bonds of sin and superstition. But that would have to wait until another visit.

On another trek, I stopped at a village far from home. The chief welcomed me and arranged for a hut near his own. I entered it after dark and went to bed. During the night I awoke and lit a lantern; then I saw the room contained many idols and altars. Had the chief deliberately put me there in the power of his village gods to protect me, or to protect himself from me? It gave me a creepy feeling so I left, and spent the rest of the night under a tree.

The next day the chief commented on my move. This led to a discussion of their gods and superstitions. Knowledge of their animistic worship passed from one generation to the next orally.

I explained that our knowledge and understanding of God came to us through a Book. They knew nothing of paper, writing, or books, so to them my Yoruba Bible would only be considered an object of worship, not a written revelation from God.

I spent several days sharing God's plan of salvation. The last night we talked late. About four in the morning I woke suddenly to hear drums and horns and people talking excitedly. Outside, I saw the reason—a comet* streaking across the sky. To them it was an evil omen, because they didn't understand it. I tried to explain it before we left early the next morning.

We walked about 25 miles, arriving at Ejiba by dark. When we asked for a place to spend the night, the chief refused. He wouldn't even give us food and water.

"What have I done?"

"Oyinbo, we don't want you in our town."

"Let's go on, it's only thirteen miles to Egbe," I told my men. As we started out single file along the trail, although I was weary, I reveled in the beauty of the night—the scent of some tropical flower, and the towering trees silhouetted black in the moonlight. As we walked, the carriers discussed the incident at Ejiba. They felt the chief and his people, after seeing the comet, feared a catastrophe; they didn't want whatever evil the presence of a white man might bring.

We reached Egbe about midnight to find my co-worker, Fred, sick with malaria. He'd been lonely and miserable, but now that I'd come, he brightened up and we talked until daylight.

*Halley's Comet, April 1910.

9. A thousand may fall

"A thousand may fall at your side, and ten thousand at your right hand, but it shall not approach you." Psalm 91:7

In Egbe town the gospel took hold rapidly. The church had been built, the believers were gaining confidence, and the Holy Spirit was mightily at work through their prayers and witness. Early in the year of 1910 there were about 50 believers. In the following months the number tripled.

On Sunday, May 29, practically every Christian in Egbe started out with us early in the morning to preach in the surrounding villages. There were 173 of us! When we got back to Egbe after preaching, over 400 people were waiting at the church for a service. When these left, the church filled up again. In the afternoon, over 800 returned for more. After the messages that day, more than 100 people made the decision to follow Jesus.

Those days, I prayed a lot. I didn't want the young believers depending on me. I sought to make them God-reliant and self-reliant.

One day I was called to help a woman in labor; the mother and child lived. After that, the husband, Oni, a Shango priest, would bring his wife and baby for medical care, and he'd listen to the gospel.

"Oyinbo," he said one day, "if what you say is true, then I'm going to an eternal fire."

By this time many believers could read and had their own Yoruba Bibles. They read them aloud in town, and Oni listened. The day came when he received Jesus Christ. Then he asked me to burn his big idol.

"No, Oni, you must destroy it yourself."

He went home, brought the idol, and set it down in front of my house. "What shall I do now?" he asked.

"Use the ax."

As the onlookers realized what he was going to do, they fled. He chopped the idol in pieces and threw it on a fire. This was the greatest victory yet in Egbe.

The people watched from a distance, expecting to see the priest die. But the idol burned to ashes, and nothing happened to Oni.

"May I sleep in your house tonight?" he asked.

I agreed. He stayed three or four nights.

"I'm a Christian now," he said. "I don't know what the people will do to me, but I'm going back to my compound."

Nothing happened. He became a great personal worker. If he had trouble helping a person understand the gospel, he'd bring him to me.

Satan, that "roaring lion," was being trod upon as God had promised!

Then Ayana came. One morning as I was eating breakfast, I heard someone shuffling up the path. I went out to greet the stranger. He'd come for medical help for an ulcer open from his ankle to his knee. The odor was terrible. All he'd brought with him was an idol under his arm.

In those days my small dispensary had no accommodation for out-of-town patients. I treated the ulcer and told him to return the next day.

E

"Sir, where will I spend the night?"

"Can't you go home?"

"Hardly," he answered. "I live beyond the Wednesday market." He hesitated a moment and then asked, "May I sleep on your veranda?"

I agreed. So for many weeks, Ayana slept on my porch, sickening odor and all.

One day when I'd finished the medical work and returned home, he said, "Oyinbo, I'm saved. Jesus has come into my heart."

I sat down and questioned him carefully. Sure enough, he knew what it was all about. He'd become a child of God.

Before supper, as I sat outside enjoying the cool air, Ayana said, "Oyinbo, I want to go to my people. Please follow me after a few days and tell them the story, because no one in my village has ever heard of Jesus."

"You tell them."

"I cannot read."

"Well, do you know you're saved?"

"Oh, yes, I know the blood of Jesus Christ, God's Son, has cleansed me from all my sin."

"That's good. Go and tell them that."

"But sir, I cannot read."

"You don't have to be able to read. Tell them what Jesus has done for you."

After supper, I invited Ayana to come inside. We talked late; I read to him from God's Word and we had a happy time in prayer together. Then he lay down right where he was and went to sleep.

About five the next morning, as I was praying, he woke up. He was soon ready to leave, and I accompanied him a piece along the trail. Then kneeling in the path, I committed him to God, and he went on his way.

Days passed, and one morning at the dispensary I looked up and saw him limping toward me.

"How is your stomach?" I greeted him.

"My stomach is bubbling over," he answered with a big smile.

After I'd finished, he told me about his visit home. "But Oyinbo," he finished, "you will go to my village?"

"Yes, after a while."

When his ulcer healed, he returned home. His brother wanted to make a thank offering to one of the family idols.

"No, I don't need any more sacrifices. While I was with Oyinbo Egbe, I received Jesus as my Lord and Savior."

This angered his brother and the leaders of the idol worship. They remonstrated. They cursed. Nothing would change his mind. Then they forcibly took him to the top of a hill and pushed him over. He tumbled down to the rocky bottom, his body bruised and the skin pierced in many places. He lay for some time in a semi-conscious state. Later, he painfully dragged himself to a shade tree to rest.

When some of the townspeople heard about it, they searched until they found him.

"What happened, Ayana?"

"My brother wanted to sacrifice to the idol for me. I don't need such sacrifices now because I'm a Christian."

These men sent a messenger to me. I went at once. As word reached Ayana that I was nearing the village, he painfully got to his feet and came to meet me, accompanied by a hundred villagers.

"Oyinbo, I'm so glad you're here at last. I've told my people all I know; they want to hear more."

My heart was moved as I looked at the large group who could neither read or write, but who'd seen the great change in Ayana's life. They wanted to know and love his Savior, too.

As a result of his testimony, three churches were established.

When I was sick with malaria, some Christians came to tell me that a British District Officer—called simply "the D.O."—had ordered six small churches demolished. I went to see him.

I asked him why this order? He replied that the chief didn't want them. Since the churches had been there before this chief came into power, I suggested that we go together to see the man. When we arrived, the D.O. asked the chief if he wanted the churches.

"Whatever you say, sir," the chief replied.

"No, the chief doesn't want them," the interpreter translated.

"You tell the D.O. what the chief said. I know your language," I said to the interpreter. He did, and the churches weren't destroyed.

Persecution flared up at Ogga, where the first baptized Yagba believers lived.

I'd already been asleep some time when I woke to hear voices calling urgently, "Oyinbo! Oyinbo!"

Going outside, I saw several young men, obviously out of breath. "Oyinbo, come quickly! They've burned our houses, and they're going to kill us!" They went on to say that the town of Ogga was in turmoil.

I dressed quickly and we started off, single file through the tall grass and bush, oblivious to the dangers of the night. When I arrived, I found about 20 believers badly beaten and shaken up. I comforted them and when the townspeople, led by their angry chief, came near I stepped forward.

"Oyinbo, we don't want these believers here," the chief shouted.

"Listen, chief, these people belong here. This is their home town. You mustn't touch them; I am going to stay here with them for a while."

There was much shouting and cursing; they called me many bad names. Finally, the group calmed down and left.

Then I went with the believers back to their smoldering homes. As I looked at their faces and saw the anxiety and anguish there, the wounds, the welts on their bodies from the beating, I thanked God He'd called me to be a missionary of the cross to bring the gospel to such dear people as these, who were willing to suffer so much for Jesus' sake.

I stayed with them for two weeks. As we repaired their huts and re-roofed them, there was ample opportunity to teach them more of the Word of God. Any place was home to me and this was where I was needed at the moment. I wanted to identify with the believers and help them.

Persecution continued there. Some of the married believers had their wives taken from them and their crops burned. Occasionally they were beaten, but the Lord strengthened them, and the more they suffered, the more they loved Him.

"Let them take all we have; let them kill us if they want. We will not deny Christ, who has made our stomachs sweet."

Christians from Ogga went to Odo Okeri where some accepted Christ. About 100 of them built a church and asked for a teacher.

From Egbe the work developed in all directions. Missionaries visited Eri and Odo Okeri every Sunday, and they wanted churches and teachers. Eri had 60 believers and 200 adherents, and Odo Okeri 100 believers and 200 adherents.

At Ejiba, there were seven professed believers for some months, and then eight more came from there desiring to know the way of salvation.

At Okuron while itinerating, we found the people observing Sunday because it was a day of rest for Oyinbo Egbe. On the same trip at Okeloke, the whole population turned out en masse to meet us, singing the Christian songs they had heard in Egbe market. This was one of the great advantages of having based our work in a market town.

I trekked in another direction and some men invited me to visit a place I'd never heard of called Odo Osin. It was miles through the bush. When I got there, I asked how they'd heard the gospel. They'd gone to markets in towns with little churches. So the word spread faster than we could keep up with it! Calls came in continually for us to visit new groups.

At Egbe, believers were requesting baptism. We decided to wait until they were thoroughly tested and proved.

Everywhere we went, people wanted to buy Bibles. Two years before, no one could read outside of the group at Ogga. Now there were about 250 reading the Bible intelligently in their own language.

The British introduced pounds, shillings and pence as currency in Nigeria about 1907, but cowries and barter continued to be in general use in the villages for a number of years. However, the people gradually realized that coins were more convenient. The anini, worth one-tenth of a penny, the halfpenny, and the penny all had holes in the center so they could be strung together on a cord and conveniently slung around the neck, as pockets weren't commonly in use.

The people worked hard to buy Bibles of their own. Even though the cost was subsidized, yet the price was high for them to pay.

Some people asked why we didn't give the Bibles free. I felt the people would value them more if they bought them.

The church in Yagbaland was in its first love, and the gospel spread from village to village like a bush fire.

10. The Lord, my refuge

"You will only look on with your eyes, and see the recompense of the wicked. For you have made the Lord, my refuge." Psalm 91:9

For two years I suffered from repeated attacks of dysentery, so Dr. Stirrett sent me on furlough in July, 1911. During the first Sunday service I attended back in Gospel Tabernacle, Hamilton, Canada, my emotions overcame me. Being in church again, hearing the music, having fellowship with old friends, overwhelmed me. And yet ever since I'd arrived in Hamilton on this my first furlough, somehow it seemed different. The welcome home was enthusiastic and warm; the assurance from people who had faithfully prayed for me was a great encouragement, but it wasn't the same as before. I guess I'd changed; I didn't feel as though I belonged any longer; my heart was back in Egbe. Before going to Africa I'd been welcomed into many homes, among them the McIntoshes'. While at Bible School, I'd spent Christmas vacation with them. I'd found that Ethel McIntosh and I had much in common. She was a pretty brown-haired girl with smiling eyes and a warm personality. I'd enjoyed her company. However, when I'd left in 1908, Ethel wasn't concerned for faraway Africa.

Now, as I sat in the congregation, Ethel seemed the most attractive girl in the choir—in the church, for that matter. Something was happening to me. Did Ethel have any idea? Probably she did. I decided to see her more often.

Under doctor's care, my strength slowly returned, but because I was still attacked by dysentery, I weighed only 100 pounds. However, the good food and fellowship in the McIntosh home began to do wonders. By now, my interest in Ethel was obvious to all.

I learned that she, Ethel Tucker McIntosh, was born to William and Mary Tucker, on April 5, 1881, in Hamilton. When quite young she'd been converted under the Rev. Herbert Mackenzie's ministry, and became a charter member of the Gospel Tabernacle. Her father died soon after; with her mother she moved to Perry, New York, where her mother remarried. Two children were born to this marriage, Lillian and Mabel, and later the family moved back to Hamilton.

Now, Ethel Tucker McIntosh, for she'd taken her stepfather's name, and I began to enjoy being together. We had long talks. Our interests seemed to dovetail nicely except that I was a missionary and my life was committed to Christ for Africa, and Ethel had no call to go there yet.

I wanted to ask her to marry me, but I couldn't, as I was returning to Africa. I remembered the constant loneliness at Egbe and how difficult it had been to communicate with the women and children. How I longed to have a companion like Ethel there with me!

When I'd been home five months, Fred Rutherford, my co-worker at Egbe, became ill and returned to Canada. I thought of the young church in Yagbaland, on their own except for a new missionary, Guy Playfair, just learning the language. I arranged an interview with our General Director, the Rev. R. V. Bingham.

"Mr. Bingham, I want to go back to Africa."

"You can't go back yet. You're not well."

"Never mind, I'm not married and no one is dependent on me; I want to go back."

"Well, I'll let you return," Mr. Bingham said, "if you'll first go to a sanitarium."

So I went to one in Battle Creek, Michigan, where they promptly cleared up the dysentery. They warned me, however, that it would likely recur, and said I should be careful. Upon my return to Toronto, I welcomed Mr. Rutherford home. We spent two long days, praying and discussing the Yagba work. Then, not long after, he, with a host of others, accompanied me to the railway station. Putting his arms around me, he said, "Tommie, I don't know if I'll see you again on earth. Goodbye, and God be with you." A few months later, back in Africa, I received word that he was with the Lord.

My journey back to Nigeria was uneventful.

The day after my arrival at Patigi, on the way to Egbe, two Yagbas came rushing into the compound. Our joy at seeing each other again was so full, we all lacked words! Half an hour later nearly 100 came singing, beside themselves with joy; I could hardly keep the tears back. We spent the day visiting together.

It was late when I got to sleep. I recalled my first night there with Dr. Stirrett, on September 5, 1908. Then I thought about those I'd so recently left in Hamilton, especially Ethel. I crawled out of bed and found paper and pen. Back under the mosquito net, by the feeble light of a storm lantern, I wrote her, telling of the great welcome and how happy I was to be back among my people.

The next day many more came. This encouraged my heart as I prepared to plunge again into the busy, yet lonely life at Egbe.

While home, a friend gave me a bicycle, so when we left Patigi, on April 25, 1912, I rode with a great host of friends, some ahead, some behind, accompanying me like an honor guard. Along the way more believers joined us from outstations.

When we approached Odo Okeri, about 17 miles from Egbe, the believers came out to greet us with four drums, and escorted us into the village with singing and music. It was here Guy Playfair met me. We had a fine meeting that night. It was great to hear their songs again.

In the morning we left for Egbe, but we hadn't been on the path long before a large group from the Eri church joined us. Their drums announced our coming. When we got within two miles of Egbe, people began meeting us with more drums and rams' horns. The nearer we got to town, the greater the crowd became. At the gate a large party of children waited, singing songs about Jesus. As we passed through Egbe, the women stood outside their compounds saluting us with their characteristic shrill calls and greetings.

The mission compound remained packed all day. At night a great crowd gathered for a tremendous time of praise and thanks to God for keeping us all and bringing us together again. The singing thrilled me especially. I had always felt that we should, instead of introducing English hymns, use tunes they already knew. The English tunes just ruin the words, as they don't fit.

My mind went back to the day I'd arrived there less than four years before. Then no one welcomed me; the people ran away, fearful. But now, in answer to prayer, their hearts had changed and they were hungry to hear the Word of God. Uppermost in my mind was the longing that my friends in Canada, who'd prayed for the work, could see this tremendous welcome the people had given me.

The next day, Sunday, a great crowd gathered by 6 a.m. and we started for the villages. Guy Playfair went in one direction; some of the believers in another; and I took a third way. About 400 men went with us. When we returned home we found that converts from several of the other churches were waiting to welcome me. In fact, people came for days.

11. Your dwelling place

"Even the Most High, your dwelling place." Psalm 91:9

The early months of my second term passed quickly. I stepped back easily into my daily schedule, doing medical work and visitation in the mornings, teaching believers and doing more visitation in the afternoons, and counselling and preaching in the evenings. Saturday afternoons I met with the Sunday School teachers, and Sundays were busy with team visits to the villages before the morning service and in the early afternoon, followed by Sunday School and the evening service.

I soon became engrossed in reestablishing the work and spent much time visiting believers in the villages. I was glad for the privilege of working with these dear people. It was almost four years since I'd first arrived in Egbe, and looking back, I praised God for all He'd done.

I found that many believers wanted to be baptized. My new co-worker, Guy Playfair, and I gave ourselves to the task of preparing them. Over a hundred attended each class. After thorough instruction, we began inviting them, one by one, to our rooms to interview them privately. We questioned them regarding every aspect of their lives and of their understanding of how a Christian should live. For example, we asked: How do you know you are saved? What is baptism? How long have you been a Christian? Have you ever tried to lead anyone to Christ? Each one said he had! Often they brought along members of their family or friends to hear the Word of God.

We set a day in November 1912 for the first baptismal service at Egbe, and invited Mr. and Mrs. Lang (he had remarried) to come from Patigi to participate. When they were within 15 minutes walk of Egbe, word spread, and by the time they reached the town gate, several hundred people had rushed to meet them. The women were beside themselves with joy as they surrounded Mrs. Lang, the first white woman they had ever seen, and they claimed her for their own. Observing their enthusiasm as they danced and sang around her, I saw the necessity of a woman to minister to them. Not only did I long for the companionship of a helpmate, now I realized the work itself needed her. Thus encouraged, I redoubled my plea to the Lord, and prayed, "Lord, that it might be Ethel!"

Sunday we woke before six to discover a great crowd already on the compound. After a hurried breakfast, we started down the trail, single-file, to the stream. Hundreds of people lined both sides of the river and stood on the banks sloping down to the water's edge. There, after singing, preaching and testimonies, 99 went into the water. Eighty-three men were baptized; they stood as a group in the water until their number was complete, then came out singing. Then 16 women followed their Lord in baptism. This was a breakthrough. These were the first fruits of the preaching of the gospel at Egbe. Now the women asked for a sister-in-the-Lord to carry them deeper into the truth that would change hearts and homes in Yagbaland.

The work grew fast; every night except Sunday the believers gathered for prayer. Their lives were completely changed; they were eager to learn to read, taking their primers and Bibles with them to study in spare moments. When they could, they read aloud to those unable to read. God used their concern for their neighbors to draw many to himself. They kept their homes neat and clean, and dressed their families in a way that honored the Lord.

One Saturday night a group came to tell me they wouldn't be in church the next morning. They planned to walk out to villages ten or twelve miles away, to witness to their people.

In the meantime, my co-worker, Guy Playfair, moved to Oro to begin a work there among the Igbominas. I continued at Egbe alone.

As I could, I continued to trek. On one trip I visited a village where some had been Christians for about two years. I asked them if they'd like Jesus to come today.

"No!" replied a young man.

"Why do you say no?"

"Well, if He should come today, I wouldn't have anyone to bring to Him."

A year later I returned to that village for a baptismal service. The first candidate was that young man. "Son," I asked him, "would you like to see Jesus today?"

"Yes, if He comes today, I have these to bring to Him." With him stood three young men.

The pastor had already instructed them, so after talking to each one, we baptized them.

I learned that the vital importance of careful examination couldn't be overemphasized. I told the church leaders that our primary desire isn't that great numbers be added to the church, but that we might be certain that those who become members were living pure lives and seeking to be true disciples of Jesus Christ.

Because many of them had been named after the idols that their parents worshiped, at their time of baptism they chose new names, frequently from the Bible. The Christians would greet them by their new names as they came up out of the water.

Polygamy presented a great problem. One man in Egbe, an outstanding believer, had three wives. When he asked for baptism, he was shown from the Scriptures that he should have but one wife. To this he agreed but the second and third wives refused to leave him. He was a kindly, old gentleman and they'd lived together many years. The women pleaded that they had nowhere to go, nor any means of livelihood. The husband concluded that it would not be a good Christian testimony to turn them out, as he had been party to their circumstances. He set them up in separate quarters; maintained them, meeting all their needs, but living only with his first wife. This problem needed much wisdom. Had the man with the three wives been accepted, baptized, and brought into fellowship with the church, it would have become a stumbling block to some who would seek other wives in the future, excusing themselves. Although in the beginning a few with more than one wife had been baptized and in fellowship with the church, this was soon altered. Polygamists were not chosen for positions of leadership in the church and were not permitted to have an active part in the ministry. The Holy Spirit, who lived within these new believers, was watching over them and guiding in the establishment of Christ's Church among the Yagbas.

Christianity adapts to every man's heart need. Much of the social and material order can be uplifted and sanctified by salvation through faith in Jesus Christ. The Christian life is by divine design the manner in which every man can live life to its fullest, richest realization. Christianity is divinely purposed to be the atmosphere in which every man in Christ can be most comfortable, most happy, best adjusted to the world about him. But it must be totally accepted, it cannot coexist with partial, incomplete, compromising commitment. It is an all-or-nothing way of life. Hence it was to be anticipated that the battle with sin and superstition would be fierce.

When young men became Christians, they found they could not obtain wives. The old men married the girls when they were eight years old. This troubled me greatly. I prayed about it and decided to do something. I went to the government officer to ask his advice as to how believers could obtain wives. He promised to investigate.

Soon, 12 of the leading chiefs from as far as 30 miles away came in a body to see me.

"Oyinbo, don't do anything more regarding girls," they said.

"You fellows have married all the eligible girls. The young Christians can't find wives, so what are they going to do?"

"We will cooperate," they replied. "They can have all the women they want, we don't care who has the women. We want the children."

"How many wives do you have?" I asked one chief.

"Sixty."

"How many live on your compound?"

"Two."

"Where are the others?"

"I don't know, and I don't care. Your young men can have all the women they want. All I want is the children."

Not long after, the Resident of the province came to Egbe and conducted a full-scale investigation into the entire matter of marriage among the Yagbas. He did much to regularize marriage relationships, while still preserving as much as possible the customs and culture of the Yagbas. The principle of dowry was enforced, and seemed to help regularize the relationship of husband and wife; a chief or leading person could no longer take a girl without the benefit of a ceremony. It resulted in a much happier and scripturally-acceptable marriage relationship among the believers.

In the early days when a young man wanted to marry a girl and didn't have the dowry money required by her father, he borrowed money. From then on he was seldom able to pay off the debt because interest was added and the debt mounted.

Eventually young men and women could choose the one they wanted to marry. Yagba custom had always required that such arrangements be made by the families of the boy and girl. Unbelieving parents steadfastly refused the new-fangled idea. So missionaries often filled the place of go-between and arranged matters between the families. More than once a boy came to me and said, "Oyinbo, do you see that girl over there? She pleases me. Would you ask her if she likes me?"

So I'd go to the girl and say, "Do you see that boy over there? He thinks you are very nice. Do you like him?"

"I'll tell you later," she would usually reply. Then after a few days she'd come and say, "Yes."

Then I would go to the girl's father and ask if he'd consider the young man a suitable husband for his daughter. If he agreed, we would then decide upon the dowry to be paid.

By the fall of 1913, many more had requested baptism. I began classes of instruction, and by November, after each had been interviewed, 116 were ready. Mr. Merryweather and Mr. Stanley came from their stations to help. On the Sunday morning at the river, we sang, then Mr. Merryweather spoke. After prayer, the three of us stepped into the water and baptized the group, three at a time. As I looked upon those dear ones following the Lord in this way, I praised God for answering the prayers of His people at home.

In the afternoon, after the usual preaching service, over 200 sat down to the Lord's Table. We spent a blessed day in the service of our King!

Mr. Stanley stayed on with me and we visited several villages. With the local leaders, we examined candidates who'd completed preparation and then baptized them; 24 young men at Odara, and six at Omi. We preached in other villages as we passed through. At Ogga, we met Dani, still patient and sweet, although sad, for recently eight of their number had died from small pox.

As we made this hurried trek, we realized how much these groups of Christians needed someone to stay with them longer to instruct and encourage them in the Word. I only wished I could.

On December 31, 1913, some 800 believers met in the Egbe church for a watchnight service. After we dismissed, the Christians went down to chief Agbana's compound and sang until morning. Then about 1200 gathered for a feast and fellowship to begin the New Year. That night I concluded the entry in my diary, "Very tired, but happy in Jesus!"

A few days later I went to visit Guy Playfair at Oro. We went to sympathize with the chief on the death of his wife in childbirth. In those days, if a mother died and left a baby less than a year old, it was buried with the mother or taken out to the bush. They had no way of keeping an orphan alive.

I once tried to pay a woman to nurse a tiny motherless infant.

"Even if you give me all the money you have, I would never nurse it," she said.

"Why?"

"If I nursed it, the spirit of the dead mother would come upon my baby or me."

When I saw they were going to dispose of the chief's baby, I asked for it. The chief consented, so they brought it to me that evening. Here I was, a bachelor, with a newborn baby. If ever I wished for a wife, I did that night.

First of all, I bathed it, then it began to cry. Fresh milk was unobtainable, but I did have tinned "cow" on the table. I thanked God for Nestle's evaporated milk that night! And for the first time, I noticed a recipe on the side of the can. That was a lifesaver. It told me how to make the formula. I prepared the milk, but how could I feed it? I searched through my belongings and found a bottle with a cork. Piercing a hole in the cork, I held the baby on my knee and shook the bottle over its mouth to let the milk drip in.

The baby choked. I didn't have a rubber nipple for the little rascal to suck on, so what could I do? I prayed. Then I remembered my camera had a rubber tube with a bulb on the end. I cut a piece of the tube and put it through the cork. Then I pierced the rubber part of a medicine dropper, joined the glass end to the tubing and, presto, the baby liked the milk and I liked the method.

I sent to Egbe for Sefi, one of the Christian women. But that night, the baby fussed until I took it in bed with me. Sefi arrived the next day and took charge. As news spread, hundreds of women came to watch her feed the baby its formula. They'd never seen anything like this before. So a life was saved. This was the first of hundreds of orphans brought to us in Yagba and Igbomina lands.

As I went about and saw the harsh treatment of young mothers and infants, I tried to stop it, but couldn't.

"You are going to kill him," I said to a woman who was force-feeding her baby.

"My mother did it to me, and I'm alive. What do you know about babies? You're not even married."

I felt helpless, but I prayed that the Lord would burden the hearts of some young women at home to come and minister to these needy women and helpless babies.

Back in Hamilton, God began to answer my prayers. At a midweek service in the Gospel Tabernacle, a missionary from West Africa told of her work. More than one young heart, Ethel's included, caught a vision of the need and responded.

After the meeting she prayed, "Lord, I believe You're calling me to Africa. If I'm wrong, then stop me. But if I'm right, then open the way and show me what to do."

Then she told Pastor Philpott and the elders. Their reaction was definite. "No, Miss McIntosh. You wouldn't last three months out there."

How could this be? She had been so sure that God had called her. She hurried home, and passed through the house up to the attic. There, all alone, she got down on her knees and prayed for guidance.

When she met with the elders again, she said, "Gentlemen, it may be that I *will* only live three months out in Africa. Nevertheless, I believe God has called me. If He wants me there for only three months, I am willing to go."

In the light of her determination, the church responded. They not only agreed to support her financially while in Africa, but promised that if she couldn't stay out there they would pay her fare to bring her home.

When I heard this good news, I wrote and proposed. She agreed to marry me, and took the next step, application to SIM.

But when the Mission doctor wrote his report, he stated his opinion that she should not go, that she would not live many months over there. He diagnosed her condition as Graves' disease, and prescribed a course of treatment. Although she improved through this treatment, the Mission director, Mr. Bingham, hesitated to send her to the tropical heat and isolation of Egbe.

But after further consultation with the church board, who renewed their assurance of support for her, Mr. Bingham agreed. Ethel prepared to sail with a party of missionaries led by Mr. Bingham and his friend the Rev. Herbert Mackenzie of Cleveland, Ohio.

This was Mr. Bingham's third trip to Nigeria. His first two had been tragic. Twenty-one years before, in 1893, he and two companions, Walter Gowans and Thomas Kent, had landed in Lagos. That day they knew nothing of what lay ahead.

The missionaries they met on the coast were pessimistic about these newcomers' plans to penetrate to the interior. The obstacles that missionaries faced were formidable. Disease and death stalked the footsteps of every white man who struggled to gain a foothold for the gospel in West Africa, then referred to as part of the Sudan.

"You wish to see the Sudan?" the Superintendent of one mission said to them. "You will never see the Sudan. Your children will never see the Sudan. Your grandchildren may."

Walter Gowans did see the Sudan, but only briefly. He penetrated the interior some 500 miles on foot and then died of malaria near Zaria, alone. Tom Kent likewise succumbed at Bida. Without recruits, support, or help at home, Rowland Bingham had been forced to abandon this venture of faith and return to Canada. In 1900 he made another unsuccessful attempt. Within three weeks of landing, he was stricken with fever and carried aboard ship and sent home again.

In 1902 a third party of four succeeded in establishing the first SIM station at Patigi. A second station was opened at Wushishi in 1904. George Sanderson and I arrived in Nigeria in 1908.

Mr. Bingham's party left Canada in November 1914. Ethel was on her way! I thought of her as the ship sailed along the west coast of Africa. She told me of standing alone on the rear deck at night looking up at the myriads of stars overhead. She watched the white foam of the ship's wake as it trailed on behind and disappeared into the night. She said she felt so small, even the ship itself seemed insignificant on the broad

F

heaving sea. Yet, God, who had brought her step by step to this moment, was near, and she felt safe in His care. He had opened the way for her and He would continue to lead as she neared Nigeria, the Yagbas, and me.

After landing in Lagos the party boarded the up-country train for Minna, which was then the headquarters for SIM, where the new missionaries would spend a year studying the language.

In those early days of the Mission, engaged couples spent the first year on separate stations, after which they were permitted to marry. So Ethel went to Minna, and I remained at Egbe, some 160 miles of bush paths away. My consolation was two letters from her, and a long talk with one of the missionaries who had traveled with her party.

12. No evil befall you

"No evil will befall you, nor will any plague come near your tent."
Psalm 91:10

Mr. Bingham was very eager to visit Egbe, the scene of the first triumph of the gospel in SIM. I spent several days getting ready for the event. When everything was prepared, I went to Patigi to meet our guests and escort them the 50 miles to Egbe. Knowing that Mr. Bingham had been so ill on his two previous visits, I arranged for him to be carried in a hammock when he became tired.

En route, we stopped the first night in a village where there were Christians. When Mr. Bingham met them, the light in his face, and the deep-seated joy expressed, had to be seen to be believed. At last, this man was looking into faces of those who had been won to Christ in answer to his prayers of faith.

We arrived in Egbe New Year's Day, 1915, a red-letter day in Rowland Bingham's life. As we neared the town, the last few miles led up a gradual incline to pass into the circle of hills bordering the town. A group of boys came running to meet us; then men and women, all neatly dressed. At the top of the hill a regular procession met us with music and greetings. In the midst of the crowd was our Christian chief, Agbana, in a hammock. He alighted to welcome us, and offered his hammock to Mr. Bingham, who declined, feeling that the taking of any preeminent place would dishonor the Lord, whose wonderful work of grace he was beholding.

Mr. Bingham's heart was too full for words as we proceeded the remaining two miles, then through the town to the mission compound, full of enthusiastic welcomers singing to the accompaniment of musical instruments. Mr. Bingham couldn't keep back the tears. He said later that he lived little in the emotional, but as he thought of the transformation in the lives of these happy Christians since my arrival seven years before, he couldn't help it. This was full compensation for the years of painful sowing.

At the house, the party sat down to rest and to receive the greetings of all who came to welcome the leader and spiritual father of the missionaries. People continued coming by the hundreds, bringing gifts and greetings.

In the evening, hundreds gathered before the house to hear Mr. Bingham speak. It was a moving scene. The believers sang with tremendous enthusiasm the new songs of the redeemed to their familiar African tunes.

Afterwards, Mr. Bingham told me how he longed that all those who by their prayers and gifts had made it all possible, could see what God had wrought! What encouragement it would give them, as it had him, to press on until a similar harvest would be gathered from other tribes in the Sudan.

He said that as he beheld this glorious scene, he thought of his companions who had so soon laid down their lives; he thought of the years of disappointment, disease and death, now all washed away with the joy that flooded his soul. He turned, put his arms around me, and wept. Not often had anyone seen him weep, but he was deeply moved and said, "Son, at last we see the first-fruits."

This visit initiated the annual Yagba Conference. Christians from dozens of surrounding villages came with sleeping mats and stayed a week. Each morning began with a pre-sunrise prayer service. The Yagba leaders and I interviewed those requesting baptism. In the evenings I interpreted for Mr. Bingham and Mr. Mackenzie as they preached.

In the afternoon of the last day of the conference, we went to the river. Dr. Stirrett and Norman Davis assisted Mr. Bingham and Mr. Mackenzie in baptizing 111 believers. Then we returned to the church, where about 700 gathered. They took a love offering equivalent to $25, to be used for the support of God's work. Mr. Bingham preached the first hour, then Mr. Mackenzie spoke about the Lord's Supper before we observed it with some 400 African brothers and sisters. It was a never-to-be-forgotten day for all.

One of the most touching incidents of their visit was the appeal to Mr. Bingham from a deputation of Christian women. They asked him if a white sister could come to teach and guide them. He told them that before the year ended, I would be marrying Miss Ethel McIntosh and bringing her to serve there at Egbe.

He also told us that when the conference was over we would all travel together to Minna, to hold the Mission's first Field Conference. I could hardly wait.

Finally we set off for Ilorin, and there boarded the train. I paced up and down the aisle, unable to stay seated. In a few hours I'd see Ethel!

I was in a world of my own as I anticipated being with her again. I stepped out on the rear platform of the train, thinking, as the iron rails spun out from under the wheels, what a difference she would make at Egbe! For nearly seven years, apart from my brief furlough, I'd lived for the most part alone there. I remembered how thrilled the women were to see Mrs. Lang. Soon I'd bring my bride, and we would serve the Yagbas together.

As the train pulled in to Minna station, I saw my Ethel waiting in the noisy crowd. Our reunion was thrilling!

The conference began the next day, and although the meetings left us little time together, we made our wedding plans—almost a year in advance!

When I returned to Egbe, my Yagba friends were full of questions about Ethel, and about our marriage customs, so very different from theirs. But there was still a long time before that great event, and I had to put my mind to the work around me.

God taught me a lesson about then that was a wonderful help to me in thinking about married life and the financial responsibilities it would involve. He reminded me again that *He* was all I needed.

Will Craig and Norman Davis served with me at Egbe. With this additional help, we opened a boarding school. Mr. Davis asked me how we'd support the school. I replied that I'd be responsible, for I counted on God's faithfulness.

"We have enough money for two weeks, then we'll have to send the students home," Mr. Davis told me one day. "Why don't you write Pastor Philpott?"

"No."

The mail messenger was leaving the next morning, so he suggested again that I write home about this need.

I did, but that night I couldn't sleep. I kept hearing God ask me, "Can't you trust me?"

Before daylight, I took that letter out of the mailbag and tore it up. The messenger left for his 200-mile trip. On his return, he brought a letter from a friend in Waterford, Ontario.

"I could not sleep last night, so I got up and wrote you a check for $200. Do you have a special need?" the man wrote.

The months passed quickly, as I helped the Christians build a new and larger church. Completing the building was quite an achievement, as we roofed it with corrugated, galvanized iron sheets, called pan. The Christians not only paid for the materials themselves, but also carried the roofing and cement by headload from Ilorin, over 80 miles away.

I also worked on a new mission house. We had received word from the government of a new ruling that said that all Europeans must locate their residences at least 400 yards from the villages—for health reasons, the order said.

I protested the ruling, as we were living in town and thought it an ideal location. But they refused to change the ruling, and I waited impatiently for the rainy season to end so I could complete the new house where I would bring my bride.

I just had time to put on the grass roof before I left for the wedding.

13. Angels guard you

"For He will give His angels charge concerning you, to guard you in all your ways." Psalm 91:11

We were married on November 22, 1915. When I arrived at Minna for the great occasion, I found that the marriage of British subjects in Nigeria had to conform to strict laws. Banns had to be posted in a public place for three weeks beforehand, generally at the Registry of Marriage Office, to announce the event and give anyone who knew of a valid reason why the marriage should not be consummated time to make it known.

The ceremony itself had to be performed in a legally-registered building, and for some unknown reason, before noon. Ethel and I complied with all the regulations, and were married in the SIM church by one of our missionaries, Norman Davis.

As we stood together to take our vows, I thought of all the obstacles that had stood in our way, and how God had removed them. I even remembered Mr. Bingham's advice not to be in too big a hurry to marry Ethel—she didn't look as though she'd last long in Africa!

Ethel was proud of the wide gold wedding band I gave her. I had arranged the purchase of that by myself. But my gift to the preacher was more hers than mine. On her way to Africa she had been given a gold sovereign while in England, and when we discussed what to give the preacher, she volunteered it.

Where it came from I don't know, but our friends had prepared roast turkey for the wedding feast, complete with a fruit cake sent out from home.

We spent our honeymoon at Paiko, a new station about 16 miles from Minna, then made preparations for our long trip to Egbe. We traveled overland to the Niger River, and then upstream to Patigi in a large dugout. During the day crocodiles and hippos lazed along the sunny banks, and birds wheeled and glided over the marshy lowlands.

At night we camped on a sand bar, using camp cots and mosquito nets. In the morning, Ethel's wedding ring was not on her finger. She must have put her hand out of the net during her sleep, and the ring, too large, fell off. She cried when she discovered the loss. We sifted through the soft sand near her cot, handful by handful, until we found it.

In the morning we arose before sunup, because by dawn we would have a crowd of people watching us brush our teeth and eat our breakfast. At Patigi we found a horse for Ethel, and I rode a bicycle. The horse was in poor shape, we soon discovered, because he had been raced most of the night. They blindfolded him before Ethel got on, for they figured if he'd seen her white face, he would have bolted. Twelve miles from Egbe the horse gave up. Ethel did the rest of the journey in a hammock, which she said she enjoyed much more.

When we were three miles from Egbe, the women all came out to meet us. They thronged the path and we couldn't move, as they all went down on their knees praising God for having sent their white sister at last. We proceeded slowly, surrounded by the women. They were weeping for joy, and so was Ethel.

As we approached Egbe I realized how long I'd waited for this day. Four years! While on furlough in 1911 I became interested in Ethel. Now God had brought us together and here she was. From that first day, Ethel's Yagba name became *Iyawo* (bride).

We escorted my bride to the small mud house with thatched roof I'd built outside the town because of the new government order.

We arrived in Egbe two days before Christmas. We didn't realize how exciting Christmas Day was going to be. As we were getting ready to go to the five o'clock service on Christmas morning, a messenger came running from the town. "Can you come quickly?" he asked Ethel. "There is a woman who needs you."

Norman Davis volunteered to go with her while I went to the church for the service.

When Ethel and Norman reached the town they were shown the house, and pulled back the mat covering the doorway. There was no window, and a cloud of black smoke poured out from the fire on the floor. Their eyes stung as they groped their way in.

There was a woman who had just given birth to twins. She had had four babies and all had died. The family and friends were waiting for the medicine man to come to take the twins away. She herself would be driven into the bush. At that time the Yagbas believed that a woman who gave birth to twins was something less than human and they wouldn't let her live any longer in the village. Believing one of the twins must be an evil spirit, the medicine man killed both to make sure.

Imagine the bravery of that mother! She held to the beliefs of her people but something gave her courage to go against custom, so she'd sent for Ethel. She looked up at Ethel from the dirt floor on which she lay and reaching out her arms imploringly, she asked, "White woman, help me. All my babies have died. I do not want to lose these. Please help me!"

Ethel realized that if they were to do anything at all they'd have to do it at once. She put the babies in a large calabash, covered them with a cloth, and urged the mother to her feet. With a woman carrying the calabash on her head, they made their way home. It was still early, and they were safely away from the town before the medicine man arrived. But the woman was in great danger, and so were we.

Church over, the people followed me home singing. I met an excited Ethel, who drew me inside to see the twins lying side by side in our wash tub.

Three days later, when Norman Davis was away, and Ethel and I were alone, a message came for me to meet a new missionary at Ilorin, 80 miles away. I didn't like to leave Ethel alone, as the town was still tense, but I didn't have much choice.

"Ethel," I asked, "are you afraid to stay alone?"

"I don't think so," she replied slowly. "I'm willing to stay."

Some of the Christian women sensed my dilemma and said, "Go, Oyinbo. We will stay here and sleep on the verandah at night."

I learned later that just a couple of hours after I left, an agitated, angry crowd had surrounded the house. In the meantime, I had stopped at Oro station and asked Mr. Donaldson to go to Egbe, as I was still uneasy. He did, and cycled around the town so everyone would know he was there. His presence must have quieted the people, and he stayed until my return.

We went from day to day expecting that the people would come to take the babies, or the mother, or possibly even burn down the house. Anything might happen. But as the days passed, the babies lived and began to grow strong. We named them Reuben and Ruth. Why the relatives of the woman didn't come and make trouble for us all, we didn't know. The only explanation was that God held them back.

Rescuing the mother and her twins and bringing them to our house was one thing. Our problems, however, were only begun. We encouraged the mother to feed the babies from her breast. This she flatly refused to do. She had come a long way in breaking one custom, but now she was unable to go the next step and break the feeding pattern.

When a mother among the Yagbas gave birth to a baby, the mother's first milk was believed to be full of worms. So for the first nine days she was not allowed to nurse her baby. In the meantime, the baby existed on a medicinal mixture prepared by the medicine man using water and unsterile utensils. The women made a funnel of their hands and poured this concoction down the baby's throat. Eighty-five percent of the babies treated thus, died. These were called "water-babies."

We tried to convince the mother, without success. Finally I told Ethel, "Put both the twins down on the floor."

"Oh, no, Tommie," she said, "I can't do that."

I insisted, then told the mother, "We're going to leave your babies there. We cannot care for them unless you're willing to feed them."

The woman begged us not to leave her and her babies. However, we walked out of the room. Seeing that we meant what we'd said, she finally picked the babies up and nursed them. That was the beginning of the emancipation of the Yagba women from the cruel treatment of mothers and twins.

The twins thrived. They got fat, their skin shone, and their eyes sparkled with good health. This dear mother would sit looking at them and say, "They are all right, aren't they?" She found it extremely hard to believe that they were, after all, normal babies, not something evil as she and the Yagba women had been told for generations.

I had tried for seven years to break this custom, only to fail. But my wife was in Egbe only two days and the Lord already had begun to use her presence to help her Yagba sisters.

We kept the babies in our room, fearful that someone would come and take them; the mother also lived in our house so that she'd be safe.

Not long after, a woman came weeping. She had had two sets of twins. They had all been disposed of by the witch doctor. She was afraid to return to her home and asked for shelter and refuge. We took her in, and she followed Ethel everywhere. This offered a wonderful opportunity for frequent testimony. It wasn't long before she opened her heart to Christ. As we were given more orphans, this woman cared for them.

Ethel studied the language daily so she could gain the confidence of the women, but teaching the mothers how to care for their babies was slow, discouraging work. At birth, the grandmother or a female relative whisked the baby away to feed it the customary "medicinal" water. When Ethel remonstrated with them they would say, "Our mothers did it to us, and we're alive."

One day a man walked past our window with a calabash in his hands. He came around to the back and when we went outside, showed us a tiny, shriveled baby.

"My wife just died. The relatives are all outside on the path demanding that I bury the baby with the mother or take it to the bush. But I have come to ask you to take him."

Another custom was being broken, and this time by a man. It seemed that God was working in His own way, making people do things even against their will.

Save it? It was nine days old, and had been fed only the "medicinal" water. He looked more dead than alive, but we took him, bathed and fed him and named him Mack after Pastor Mackenzie, who'd led Ethel to the Lord. The little lad grew strong.

The old wives watched and gossiped. They predicted that dire consequences would follow the reckless disregard of customs practiced by their mothers and grandmothers.

Ethel had no medical training, but her heart was full of compassion for the mothers and babies of Yagbaland. So she worked gladly, but with no facilities.

I built a small thatched hut near our house where she could help the women who came. One rule of this new "Maternity Center" was that the mother must stay long enough after the baby's birth for the baby to begin to grow strong and healthy. This proved to be a wise rule. Soon the husbands began bringing their wives to the compound for their deliveries. The husband would put up a shelter for his wife; would bring her food; and a relative would stay with her to help. The Christian husbands were loud in their praise of the healthy babies their young wives brought home from the mission compound.

Then God blessed *us* with a family. Ethel gave birth to our firstborn on December 5, 1917, at Egbe, assisted by Mrs. Lang and me. All went well, and we named him Clarence Herbert. The people called him *Omo Egbe*, "the child of Egbe." He was the first baby born to SIM missionaries in Yagbaland.

In August 1918, with World War I still raging, we went on furlough. We had to wait in Lagos for 10 days because so many on board ship had the flu. Finally we boarded, and the captain put up a hammock on deck for Clarence, to keep him away from the sick ones.

The trip took eight weeks, but all through this time of danger we had a sense of being kept safe by God. Two passengers died and were buried at sea, and the ship could have been torpedoed at any time. When we finally slipped into New York harbor, the captain said, "Thank God we made it!"

The flu epidemic was very widespread. In Hamilton, Ethel's youngest sister had died of it. Almost every day we watched funeral processions pass down our street.

The next spring, on March 29, 1919, Ethel gave birth again. To our amazement and the evident glory of God, we were the proud parents of twins! How gracious of Him to give us such a gift to take back to Yagbaland!

There was a boy, Emerson, and a girl, Edith—the perfect combination for preventing prejudice against girls, and giving prestige with a son. They were tiny, weighing not much more than seven pounds together, and for a while it was doubtful whether Emerson would live. But, as part of God's plan in our lives to help our Yagba friends, he survived.

14. They will bear you up

"They will bear you up in their hands, lest you strike your foot against a stone." Psalm 91:12

During our furlough, Ethel and I told of God's blessing at Egbe, especially in the maternity work. We told about the thatched hut we'd put up for women to live in when they came to us at the time of their delivery. We were excited about the fact that the babies born there were not given facial markings—a radical break with the past. If a child near Egbe had no facial markings, you knew where it had been born.

The maternity center's reputation was spreading fast. "If you want a fat baby, go to the mission," was the saying. But the facilities were so

79

poor that I had hopes of building something better. I told our friends that I could put up a "hospital" for $100. The money was promptly given, and when I returned to Egbe in December 1919, that was my first job.

I went back alone, giving Ethel and the twins time to gain strength and health. Hundreds of people came to welcome me, and for the first few days the house was packed. The great question was, "Where is Iyawo? When is she coming?"

They seemed satisfied when I told them she'd come in a few months, maybe June, but, oh, I was certainly lonely. I missed my family; I wouldn't have left them if it hadn't been for the Lord's work.

I had "Sandy" Sandercock working with me, so I lost no time in putting up the "hospital" so it would be ready when Ethel came. It was a simple structure with small sections for 16 women. I tarred the mud brick walls to protect them from the rain and the termites, and it was immediately labeled "the black house" by the Yagbas.

In August 1920, enthusiastic crowds welcomed my Iyawo and the children back. Soon she was as busy as ever with expectant mothers and people with all sorts of diseases. Fortunately, she had help from some of the schoolboys, for a small wage, with keeping the house and watching our children during the day.

One of her first jobs was reorganizing the household. She cleaned the house from top to bottom and put everything in order. Then she began to train my cook, who didn't appreciate that too much. It took a while for him to become reconciled to having Ethel in "his" territory.

Then she didn't approve of my pet monkeys. Before I was married I was lonely and they were good company. They were cute little things, gray with white around their faces, just like kittens. They used to go into the market and steal bananas. Sometimes they'd eat them, sometimes bring them home to me; I'd have to pay the owner of the bananas, of course. They liked to sit on the corner of the table when I was eating. But when Ethel came, she didn't approve. If they grabbed a salt or pepper shaker, they'd hide it and we'd never find it again. Ethel insisted I get rid of them, so I gave away two and kept one. We tried to keep him tied up.

When the twins were small, we put them to sleep on either end of the veranda. Ethel always tied up the monkey before she put the twins out, but often he'd get loose, dart down and shake first one carriage and then the other, waking the babies and making them cry. Then he'd sit on a limb of a nearby mango tree and watch Ethel try to get things quieted down again. But even though he was mischievous, we couldn't help liking the little rascal.

Because we had no way to keep meat from spoiling, the cook would prepare a fresh chicken every day. The ordinary cattle couldn't live in that area because of the tsetse fly; there was a small variety, but it was in great demand for sacrifices.

In 1921, the Lord sent Miss Merle Watson to help in the school work. She and a young African taught about 50 students. We prayed that many of these would consecrate their lives fully to the Master's service. Six of our young men in charge of village churches came in every week, some walking as far as 12 miles and arriving before 8 a.m., they were so eager to attend school. In addition to the regular subjects, we gave them material for at least one of their Sunday services.

We'd outgrown our second church building, so during my year on furlough, the Christians had been busy collecting money for a larger one. We all worked together; the men made the bricks and carried the cement, whitewash, and sheets of pan for the roof as headloads for a distance of about 80 miles. I laid the bricks and did the cement work.

At that time the church members numbered 468, with eight evangelists in the field and more eager to be trained. Besides investing $900 in building materials, the Egbe believers gave $175 to support their evangelists during that year.

We made plans to dedicate the church on June 5, 1921. Invitations were sent to surrounding churches, and visitors were entertained by the local families.

The day began at 5 a.m., when we all met for prayer, then separated, visiting different sections of town. At 9:30 they marched together through town before the morning service. As they walked they sang joyfully to one of their own tunes: "Come ye unbelievers, believe on Jesus! Come all ye people of the Yagba tribe, believe on Jesus!"

The building, seating about 900, filled up quickly. The afternoon service, including those on the outside, must have numbered about 1200.

The Christians gave a love offering to the Lord that afternoon that amounted to $80. God was teaching them the joy of giving—four years earlier that was about as much as they had given during the whole year.

The church records show that between 1917 and 1921 their annual giving increased well over seven times.

Those were busy, happy days. We not only built the new church and the "black house," but also put up a new school building and a large house for single women missionaries.

Ethel wrote a letter home telling about her work with the women:

Now I must tell you that the work amongst the women is most encouraging. But so much I'd like to do is left undone because there is too much for one woman. We have a splendid women's meeting every Monday afternoon and the numbers are steadily increasing. Many take part, either reading Scripture, giving a testimony or leading in prayer. And they are growing in grace; some, who a short time ago were cold and dead spiritually, now are coming out into the Light and living near God.

We have quite a few sick children brought in daily. . . . We can reach more women through the sick children than in any other way. This gives us an opportunity to invite them to the church and most respond. Some stay on the compound awhile, so we have a better chance to reach them.

Right now we have three orphans with us. Their mothers died when they were born, and they would all have died with them if we had not taken them in. We have become very attached to them. The oldest, Mack, is nearly six; a fine little boy, and our children think a great deal of him. He and Clarence are great pals. The other two orphans are small, having been brought to us since I returned. They are both bottle-fed. I prepare the food and we have a Christian woman caring for each child.

We surely are pressed on every side, and seldom get a minute to ourselves. We often long for a little time of quiet without interruptions. But Africa is not the place to expect that. It is a comfort to know that it is for Jesus' sake, and it is a pleasure to minister to these people for whom our Lord died.

I am often alone, for Mr. Titcombe goes somewhere nearly every week, and I never know just what to expect while he is away. A short time ago, when he went to attend a conference, he had not been gone two hours when a fire broke out in the kitchen roof, and it was completely destroyed in a few minutes. I was so thankful that the flames did not reach the main house. Truly the Lord delivers us from dangers seen and unseen.

What do you think I am doing now? I have started a sewing class for young women. Why? We are anxious to reach these young girls and win them for Christ. I am pleased to say a good number are already Christians and attend regularly. . . . The time has come when we must do something to free them from the influence of the superstitious old women, for our hope is in the coming generation.

We are praying that the Lord will pour out His Spirit upon these dear people, that they may be quickened in their spiritual life. There seems to be the same tendency out here as there is at home—coldness of heart. We surely are in the last days, and it is the same all over the world.

After the new maternity hospital had been in use for some time, a government doctor came out from Ilorin to inspect it.

"Where is the hospital?" he asked.

"This is it."

"Do you mean to tell me," the doctor said, "that I've come all this way to see *that*?" He'd trekked for two days to get there.

"Wait a minute, doctor, let's go inside." We escorted him into the building, walking over and around mothers and babies everywhere.

"I don't understand this at all. We have a beautiful hospital in Ilorin, and yet we've never been able to get mothers to come. Here, your building is full."

"Doctor," I replied, "we can explain that. This little place is built on love and the Word of God. The gospel is preached and many mothers become Christians through my wife's ministry. In all our work we have but one purpose—to tell these people about God's love for them in Jesus Christ."

Back in Ilorin, he gave his report to the District Medical Officer, who, in turn, filed a very favorable report with the Director of Medical and Sanitary Services for the whole country. The DMO also wrote to the SIM Secretary in Canada, saying, "We have so far failed to do any work of any consequence among the women and children of the country as they will not come to our hospitals and dispensaries. It seems to me the next best to assist those who succeed where we have failed, and I trust that my report may result in some assistance from Government. I think very highly of this work that is being done and am greatly impressed with the help it must be towards bringing people to the feet of Jesus, which is surely the primary object of all mission effort."

Clarence and his friend Mack, the orphan a little older than himself, played together and Mack often shared his food with his friend. One afternoon, Clarence discovered a large cobra behind a desk in the living

G

room. He called me, and I had a young African bring a pole to drive it outside and kill it.

Another time Clarence got away from his baby-sitter and went out into a corn patch behind the house. He saw what he thought were dogs; he was rescued from a pack of baboons before they harmed him.

God faithfully kept the children and us "in all our ways."

We had much to thank the Lord for in those days; the·work grew in answer to prayer. Every church went forward, and although this meant more work and anxiety, we learned again that our sufficiency was not of ourselves, but of God.

I haven't mentioned the weather, but the months of intense heat before the rains began in April were especially trying. At the end of the dry season, frequent tornadoes announced the coming of the wet season. Before a tornado, the atmosphere was oppressive, without even a breeze. Then the storm broke, usually with severe wind, thunder, lightning and heavy rainfall. It was during the hot, dry spell that we longed to get away for a brief rest.

In April 1922 we took up a special offering to support the Yagba teachers. The previous year this offering had amounted to $655; this time it was $1045. As our staff of trained men increased, the offering for their support increased, too.

We praised the Lord for the fine young men he'd given us. So many of them had really stood the test. Their stories were thrilling.

There was Andrew Ayodele, for one. He was from Ejiba. I had led the first Ejiba convert to the Lord while on the road one day. He won Andrew. When Andrew learned to read, he taught other young people of the town. His family, who were witch doctors, became angry.

When they went to their farm, Andrew would climb a certain tree instead of resting with the others during the heat of the day, and study his primer secretly. When they discovered this, they smeared poison on the tree trunk. Andrew soon developed ulcers on his legs and thighs. When they became severe, he crawled to the home of his Christian teacher for help. There he heard of plans to kill him, and the teacher helped him get to us at Egbe.

Then there was Olayemi, one of the very first believers. When I first met him he was studying to be a herbalist and witch doctor. He used to come to our nightly meetings. One night I challenged him.

"Olayemi, do you ever ask things from your gods that you don't receive?"

"Yes, I've asked for many things and haven't gotten them."

I challenged him to leave idol worship for one month, and instead, in Jesus' name, ask the living God for those same things. He agreed to ask God for his three impossible requests:
1. for a certain girl; both his parents and her parents opposed him.
2. for a robe.
3. for healing for three sick friends.

God answered all three requests, and he trusted in the living God as his Lord and Savior. He was baptized with the first group in 1912, and from then on was called Moody.

Another was Bello. I had gone to his village of Ogbe, but the chief had not welcomed us and the people threw stones at us as we went about preaching. Bello, though, was interested and followed me to Egbe to hear more. He and his friend Ajere became believers, but when they returned home the chief put them in prison. They remained true. They won others, and soon built a small church.

Peter Aloko was another one of the first Christians. His faith in God was so beautifully simple that when our missionary Will Craig went to open a new station at Isanlu Makutu, Peter went with him and worked without pay for a year, saying that God would care for him. He was a faithful evangelist, walking from village to village, greatly esteemed by the people, who appreciated his simple, clear presentation of the gospel.

The growth and strength of these Christians was reflected in the churches that sprang up around them. They were so eager to learn more, and so willing to follow Christ. And once they saw a truth, they stayed with it. I was determined from the beginning that the Yagbas should assume their responsibility to build their churches and support their pastors themselves. It was true that the gospel had come to them by the lips of a missionary, but it wasn't *his* gospel—following Christ was a new relationship with God that enabled them to live for His glory right in their own land and culture.

The church at Mopa was an example of how I helped them learn to carry their responsibilities. Mopa was the place where I had visited several years before and caused consternation by interrupting a ritual sacrifice. A young man had come to me in the night, after I had preached to an empty village, and I had led him to the Lord. Since then the gospel had taken root there, and a small church had been built.

When I went back on this occasion I was welcomed by the believers. They gathered to share a problem with me.

"How can our teacher earn his living when he is so busy teaching us and our children?"

"I'm weary," I told them. "And it's late. Let's talk about it in the morning."

I prayed for hours that night, asking God to show me how to help this group get off to the right start. He did.

Next morning was Sunday, so we gathered in the church to worship together. I based my message on Malachi 3:10: "Bring ye all the tithes into the storehouse, that there may be meat in mine house." I showed them from the Bible that since they'd received the blessings of the gospel, they should assume responsibility for the testimony there. I asked if they'd be willing to give a certain number of cowrie shells each month to help support their teacher.

Two men stood. As they did so, others began to speak out, saying it was impossible. Then I asked how many would be willing to give the equivalent of five cents a month? The two remained standing, but none joined them. When asked about giving two cents a month, half the group rose. Victory came when the rest stood, indicating they would give one cent (150 cowrie shells) a month.

"Fine, I will sit at the door after the service, and receive your offerings."

Many weren't prepared, so brought their gifts to the afternoon service. They gave enough that day to support their pastor for three months. This proved to them that although they were poor, they could provide for their leader. It was a matter of teaching. I was convinced that since they used to pay their witch doctors and make sacrifices to their idols, the believers could now learn to stand behind their leaders.

As the Spirit of God moved throughout the tribe, souls were born into the Kingdom. Groups of believers gathered to sing and pray, and they built small "Houses of God" where they met to worship.

I was always sorry, however, that the old Shango priest, Daeke, never became a Christian. From the start, he tried to get rid of me; by poison, by rousing the animists, by working with chief Asalu of Egbe, but God protected my life. The day came when the tables were turned. I heard a commotion so went to the door. Daeke was running toward me with a great crowd following close behind.

"Oyinbo, save me!" he cried, rushing into the house.

"We want Daeke!" the crowd shouted.

"Why?"

"There are three dead women in town, and we're sure he poisoned them."

"Go home," I told them.

"No, Oyinbo, we want Daeke."

"No, Daeke came to me for help, he is here in my house and you cannot touch him now." After a lot of talk, I persuaded them to go back to town.

Then I turned to Daeke, lying on the floor, shaking with fear. "Daeke," I said, "you've done everything you could to destroy my life. Why have you come to me for help?"

"Oyinbo, have mercy on me."

"Yes, I'll have mercy, but what makes you think you deserve it?"

I took advantage of the opportunity to talk to him of Jesus; he never wanted to listen. This time he did, but as far as I know, he didn't receive Jesus Christ as his Savior. After this he became my "mouth" friend, but not sincerely from his heart.

I confess I had some fun at his expense. He was the most curious person and wanted to examine everything. After I acquired a motorcycle, he came to inspect it.

"Oyinbo, I'm sure the devil is in that!"

I went to my workshop for a chisel, put the motorcycle on its stand, started the engine, and told Daeke to do exactly as I said. Putting the chisel in his hand, I motioned for him to touch the sparkplugs. The spark jumped and he felt the jolt. He screamed and ran for his life. His yelling brought a huge crowd to see what was going on. They wanted to try this new game; a great source of fun and laughter as they watched one another.

Another day I showed Daeke how to sit on the pillion behind my seat. There was no seat or pillow to absorb the bumps. When I started the motor, he clung around my waist and off we went through the village, over every rough spot and rut I could find.

"I'm going to die," he moaned as he got off. The people were delighted to see him walk painfully away.

He was a frequent visitor, occasionally sitting in on an evening service in the church, but never showing genuine signs of response.

I spent more and more time visiting the villages, leaving Ethel and the children at Egbe. However, one day I told them I was going to Koro.

"Daddy, can we go?" the twins asked.

"Go and ask your mother."

"Yes, let's all go," Ethel replied.

The older boy, Clarence, got into the hammock with his mother. I took the twins with me. The children didn't speak much English at that time, but they were able to communicate with the Yagbas, young and old, in their language.

Arriving at Koro, I told the children to go and play with the village children while Ethel and I went for a walk.

We went through the town gate and outside the wall saw a heart-breaking sight. About 75 clay pots were scattered over the ground, each containing the bones of twin babies.

Returning to the village, Ethel went into the hut assigned to us and sitting down, began to weep.

"What's the matter, honey?"

"Just think, Tommie," she answered, "if I'd been born here, my babies would be out there." Ethel, too broken to face anyone, her heart grieving for the Yagba women and their children, stayed for some time, praying for them.

An old man came along to greet us. I began to talk to him about the Lord Jesus, but he didn't seem to understand. Then little Edith came skipping along and I said, "Edith, greet the old man."

"*Oku, baba!*"

The old man covered his mouth with his hand in amazement. Then her twin brother ran up and he, too, greeted the man, "*Oku, baba!*"

"Are they twins?" the old man asked in amazement.

"Yes, they are."

"They're human!"

"Of course, they're human," I assured him. "And here is their mother, do you see? She is human, too."

The old man shook his head, and slapping his hands, exclaimed, "We have always thought that when a woman gave birth to twins, she wasn't human."

There were many things that still troubled us deeply, even though we we had become accustomed to seeing cruel and ignorant practices. One day in Egbe I was visiting when I heard someone calling to me, "Give me food."

I turned around and saw a man, skin and bones, with both wrists bound in irons, tied to an upright log buried in the ground. His mind was affected, but apparently he wasn't dangerous. He asked me, "Oyinbo, will you free me? I want to lie down." I released him, and attended to his mangled wrists. Doing things like that sometimes provoked antagonism, but my heart would not let me ignore such suffering, and as I committed such actions to the Lord, I trusted Him to eventually work them out to His glory.

But my heart grieved as I thought of some people at home who had suggested that we shouldn't come and "help" these people, because they seemed so satisfied the way they were.

By 1923, Egbe seemed to be a new town. The Christians had built new homes with doors and windows. Some even had corrugated iron roofs. There was a tidier, healthier look to the town.

The new church, completed two years before, was already too small. Saturday night became known as "Believer's Night." Lively singing and testimonies were shared by Christians old and young, whose lives revealed the presence of the Holy Spirit.

Not only had hundreds been baptized, but hundreds of others had made professions of faith in Jesus Christ, and everywhere the Christians helped one another to read so they could own their own Bibles.

The Christians, more than the missionaries, were propagating the gospel, out of love for their new-found Savior.

15. You will tread upon the lion

"You will tread upon the lion and cobra, the young lion and the serpent you will trample down." Psalm 91:12

One day on trek, I entered the village of Lofin.There in the market-place I saw witch doctors disguised with grotesque masks, gathered in the center of a milling crowd. The noise was deafening; they were dancing and shouting to the accompaniment of intricate drumming. I pushed into the mob to see what was happening. When they shoved aside to let me pass, I was shocked to see a young girl lying stiff as a board, horizontal to the ground, but about two feet above it. She was perspiring profusely and foam oozed from her mouth. Being under the control of demons, she was oblivious to everything. I'd heard about this but hadn't seen it before.

I became aware of an oppressive, strange feeling, and my amazement grew when I realized that this power that controlled her was defying the law of gravity. I just had to do something; in fact I was so shaken, I forgot to ask the Lord what He wanted me to do. Instead, I touched the girl's body. It was as though I'd touched a live wire. I became drenched with sweat and felt as though I was going to be crushed to death. "Jesus, deliver me from this awful power!" I cried.

The mob howled to see the servant of God defeated. I realized I'd brought this on myself by stepping into this situation in my own strength. Then I remembered the word of the Lord, "Not by might, nor by power, but by my spirit. . ." (Zech. 4:6)

I was badly shaken. As a child of God I realized the demons couldn't have unchallenged power over me, but God had permitted this to teach me a lesson. In the midst of pandemonium, peace returned to my troubled heart. Withdrawing from the crowd, I sat under a tree and turned to God's promises in Isaiah 41:10 and 13. They had helped me many times. Then I read Mark 16:17: "In my name shall they cast out devils."

"Lord, what shall I do now?" I prayed.

"Fear not, Tommie, I will help you."

I stood, not rushing this time, but praying every step of the way as I returned. The crowd parted, still laughing and jeering. I knelt down beside the girl and prayed, "Lord, deliver this girl from the bondage of demonism, in Jesus' name."

At once the girl dropped to the ground, limp. I picked her up and carried her to a nearby hut and laid her down. The crowd roared after me. I turned and said, "Remember, my God, who has delivered this girl from the demons, is standing by my side." Hearing this, they went outside the town to a sacred idol grove.

The girl lay quiet, still unconscious. I sat beside her, praying silently, when she suddenly asked, "Where am I?"

"It's all right," I told her. "The Savior whom I worship and serve has delivered you out of the bondage of the demons."

My three companions and I slept outside that hut for three nights so that the people couldn't get to her. On the third night, I had the joy of leading that girl to saving faith in Jesus Christ.

When she had fully recovered, I arranged for two Christian couples to escort her to Oro Girls School.

So, with God's help, His servant trod upon Satan's attempt to destroy this young life.

This was not an isolated case. In another village where the gospel had never been heard before, I came upon a group in the process of their Satan worship. They would jump up in the air and remain there with nothing to support them.

Another time, in another village, I heard a voice crying, "Hunger is killing me!" I entered the hut and rushed out again. The odor was beyond description. Taking a deep breath, I reentered to see a young man with his legs fastened to a big log. There maggots crawled in the wounds on his arms and legs.

I asked an old woman sitting outside, "What is the meaning of this?"

"He is my son," she replied. "The witch doctor says he has a demon and that I must starve it out of him."

This mother had spent her life placating evil spirits. The mediator between her and the spirit world, the witch doctor, must be obeyed. So she sat and watched her son, Jegede, starve to death.

He looked up into my face, his hollow, sunken eyes pleading, and said, "Oyinbo, I am so hungry. Will you give me something to eat?"

"Yes, I will."

I turned to the mother and asked her to unfasten the boy from the log. She refused to do so, so I did.

She remonstrated with me piteously, "Oh, Oyinbo, don't do that! If you loose him it will be far worse for me, far worse for every member of my family. We will all die!"

"No, mother, neither you nor they will die. Come with me, all of you, to my house."

I couldn't carry the boy myself, so I got several others to help me take him to the mission compound. We spent hours bathing and cleansing his body and the festering wounds. He had been so long without food we had to be careful at first. Gradually, with care, he began to recover.

Poor Jegede lost his mind through this experience. I never knew whether he understood the gospel or not. He continued, after he got well, to come to greet us and we fed him. Although he could never work, we sought to treat him with compassion. He always called my wife "mother." On moonlit nights, Jegede would wander in the countryside, singing something no one else could understand.

16. Because he has loved Me

"Because he has loved Me, therefore I will deliver him." Psalm 91:14

One hot midday as I lay resting, someone called. The village lazed too. No one stirred in such heat. I'd dozed off to sleep, and at first I thought I must be dreaming. But no, I did hear a husky, muffled voice. The slight breeze carried an unpleasant odor, too.

"Who's there?"

The answer came on two feet as a man badly diseased with leprosy, drunk and dishevelled, stumbled into the room. I asked his name and why he'd come, but stupor overcame him and he slumped down on the floor in a heavy sleep. The odor and condition of the man drove me outside. Later, he awoke, confused. When he realized he was in my house, he was ashamed. I took advantage of the opportunity to speak to him of the love of Jesus. This was my first encounter of many with Ile.

93

Ile's condition worsened until his ears and nose were destroyed. It became most unpleasant for those sitting near him in church. The leaders asked me to suggest that he sit outside, so as not to offend others. This was one of the most difficult assignments I ever had. But Ile wasn't offended. After that, he sat under a tree and listened.

In April 1922, Rev. A. W. Banfield of the British and Foreign Bible Society visited Egbe. He spoke at a Sunday morning service, telling of the work and needs of the Society. The believers listened intently as he told them how the Word of God was being translated and printed for different tribes.

When I asked the congregation if they would like to have a part in this important work, they all rose, signifying their wish to share the gospel with others.

Ile sat, as usual, under a tree listening, too.

At the close, one of the elders asked, "What can we do to help?"

"Well, we've just printed the Jebba Gospels. It cost $150. You could help pay for this."

Disappointed, the elder sat down. That was a lot of money.

Immediately another stood and asked, "Would you have to have the money now, or could you give us some time?"

Mr. Banfield assured him they could have a couple of months.

Satisfied, the people dispersed. A few minutes later I heard Ile's husky voice outside, "Oyinbo, Oyinbo."

I went outside, and as I approached he asked, "Oyinbo, will you help me sell my garden plot?"

"What for, Ile?"

"I want to help the Jebba people have the Word of God."

"No, Ile, I couldn't do that."

Two months later, when the believers met to gather the offering for the Bible Society, as I neared the church, a hoarse voice called me. I walked over to Ile sitting under a big shade tree. I was alarmed to hear his weak, rasping voice, and to see how poorly he looked lying prone on the ground. He raised himself on his elbow and said in a whisper, "Oyinbo, please come close."

Ile fumbled in his ragged garment and brought out a strip of cloth on which he'd strung a number of coins. He held it out to me.

"Ile, what's this?"

"I sold everything. Take it. I want to put it in the offering because of what Jesus has done for me. Since I can't go inside the church, will you give it to Jesus?"

He placed the string of coins in my hand. It touched my heart. As I walked into the church, I noted that his gift to God was the equivalent of 75 cents.

This sacrificial gift, together with the offering collected in the church, was enough, and began a new era in the Yagba church as they realized their responsibility to share the gospel with other tribes.

Not long after this, I was called to go to Ile. Upon entering his humble hut on the edge of town, I found him lying on the bare ground, his head pillowed on his bent arm. When I spoke to him, he opened his eyes.

For some time he hadn't been able to close his mouth, so distorted was his face. Now as he recognized me, a wry half-smile wrinkled its way across his face. He couldn't speak audibly, but I read in his eyes that the gospel had made all the difference to him in this life, and for the world to come.

A few days later, Ile was with Jesus.

17. I will set him on high

"I will set him securely on high, because he has known My name." Psalm
91:14

"Where do you think you're going, sir?"

"I'm on my way to Heaven, officer," I replied to the burly policeman
glowering down at me.

"Well, you'll get there sooner than you think if you drive like that!"

I was in the wrong, but when I told him politely that I wasn't long
home from Africa, he let me off with a warning.

I drove on, my mind whirring. His jesting remarks led to serious
thoughts as I sped down the highway to the town where I was to speak
that evening.

"Yes," I thought, "the Yagbas are pretty bad off for someone to help
them, so I should be more careful."

By early 1923, Ethel and I were so worn out that Dr. Stirrett advised us to go on furlough. I suffered from chronic malaria, and Ethel was weakened by general debility due to the climate. We had two weeks to pack and get to Lagos to sail for home on May 11th.

Back in Canada eight weeks later, we settled in Hamilton, near our home church. The children especially had many adjustments to make. First of all, no one spoke Yagba!

As furlough ended, Ethel and I faced the most difficult prospect yet—that of leaving our children in the care of others so that we might return to the land and work to which God had appointed us. In those days, that was the accepted pattern. We were burdened and perplexed; our hearts tugged in two directions. The seeming conflict—the call of God pulling one way, and the demand to care for our precious children, the other. We prayed much to find the Lord's will. Then God gave us peace as we made plans to leave our children in Canada and return to Yaghaland.

In making this decision, we wouldn't tolerate for a moment the suggestion that we loved our children less than other parents loved theirs. It was our overwhelming conviction that because we were willing to be separated as a family for a while, God would make this up to all of us. In those days, there was no other way for Africa's millions to hear of God's love for them, unless we and others went to tell them.

We left in September 1924, grateful to our dear friends, Mr. and Mrs. Archie Burton of Hamilton who, without a family of their own, opened their hearts and home to our children, Clarence, almost seven, and Edith and Emerson, five and a half years.

Back at Egbe by October, in the busy days of missionary life, we found that the Lord supplied the needed grace. There were outstations to visit, sermons to preach, Christians to be taught; and I sat many hours with the elders listening to and settling *palavers* between believers, or disciplining others when they fell into sin.

As the Word was preached, the Spirit of God convicted souls of sin; multitudes believed and were added to the churches.

A new, 40-bed maternity hospital was being built, and took many hours, as I did the bricklaying.

Ethel continued to help mothers and babies. In the old, outgrown center babies were born at all hours. Ethel instructed young mothers in the care of their babies, and made sure each patient heard the gospel. As news of the work spread, many women came from distant villages. Some of them had lost two, three, four or more babies. When they left Egbe with healthy happy babies on their backs, their joy was boundless.

Other mothers, who had delivered in the villages, would bring their infants who had been fed according to the traditional way, in a dying condition. Only the strongest survived.

When women came to Ethel for help, she required that they obey her rules. After years of patient teaching and sacrificial work, the baby scene around Egbe was changed. In fact a government official credited *her*, when he found that the population in our area had doubled in ten years!

Ethel prepared the formula for the babies. Then there was our growing family of orphans. Under her supervision, older women carried them on their backs and lived on the compound. In addition to the maternity work, about 70 outpatients a day received treatment. Serious cases had to be sent to the government doctor 80 miles from Egbe. It was time Egbe had a doctor and nurse, so we prayed.

As I made out the annual report at the close of 1925, I thanked the Lord for all He had done.

The Egbe church with the 42 little churches planted in other towns and villages, gave $1500 to missionary work; $150 to the Bible Society, and $80 for training evangelists. I praised God that these churches were completely indigenous. They had never received money from the Mission for church buildings or the support of their pastors and evangelists. At Egbe, God called 27 young men to prepare for His service at the School of the Prophets under Mr. Donaldson's instruction. Eighteen others were to follow soon.

By the autumn of 1926, Ethel was too weary to continue and she returned to Canada. Malaria and other tropical diseases had sapped her strength. She entered hospital upon arrival. After regaining her strength, she made a home for the children.

At Egbe, the work developed; others were added to the missionary staff, and 70 students enrolled in a combination day and boarding school taught, among others, by David Adeniyi, the lad from Ogga who'd been given to me in 1908.

In 1927 God chose David, now a trained leader, to become the pastor of Egbe church. How my heart rejoiced!

I went on furlough that year, too. It was great to be reunited with the family; but after a year my heart yearned to get back to Africa. But when Ethel had a physical examination, her doctor concluded that she could not resume her work in Africa. It was a time of great testing as the Lord required us to go a step further and deny ourselves the joy of being together. Ethel wrote Mr. Bingham:

At your request I am writing, that you may know my mind regarding Tommie going back to the field.

We have prayed much and sought the Lord's guidance in the matter. We both believe it is the Lord's plan for him to return to the work.

First, because he is needed so much, and secondly, because he feels called to go back, and knowing this I would not dare hinder him. I am perfectly willing that he go, and I do not say this hastily.

I have counted the cost and I think I know what it will mean to me, but in spite of all that may be ahead, I can trust God. Hitherto the Lord has helped and He has never failed when I have trusted Him in hard places. There is no dread when I know that I am in His will, and I know that He will be my all.

I knew it would be a time of great loneliness for both of us, but in July 1929 I returned alone.

I returned to a very different Egbe. Now there was an African pastor, evangelists, teachers, and a number of other missionaries sharing the ministries of evangelism, church growth, education and medicine. I was thrilled to be a part of the miracle of Yagbaland. However, in August 1930, I became critically ill and returned to Canada, never again to live in Nigeria.

H

PART THREE
Tommie shares his fire
1930-1968

18. I will honor him

"He will call upon Me, and I will answer him; I will be with him in trouble; I will rescue him, and honor him." Psalm 91:15

Back in Canada, Tommie regained his strength, but the doctor would not let him return to Nigeria. God led him into a most effective ministry at home, as a representative of SIM.

For the next 28 years, Tommie was to travel across the United States and Canada, presenting the work of SIM and urging others to go and give and pray for missions. His sense of humor sparkled even in the most dignified moments. On a visit to Great Britain in 1936, he described a solemn service in a large, old church: "The church was well filled, and the pulpit away up in the air. My eyes were level with the gallery, and I looked down on the congregation. I felt like a rooster sitting on his perch ready to crow."

Tommie did not spare himself at home, even as he had not spared himself in Africa. "I have spoken forty-three times in these four weeks," he reported on one occasion. He was so much in demand that he was booked up for months, sometimes years, in advance. "It is our conviction that you are especially able in the Lord to cut away the indifference, passionless spirit, and deadness," wrote one pastor to Tommie. "Please don't spare anything, as directed by the Holy Spirit. We need to be turned right side up."

Although Tommie was away from home most of the time, he loved his home and garden very much. "Coming home was always a great experience for him, and us," the children recalled. "He always brought a gift for mother, but she'd tuck it away and say it was too nice to use!"

Roses were his favorite flower, and he grew them everywhere. He enjoyed each day that he could bring in a rosebud for Ethel.

Family life wasn't normal, with Tommie away so much, but it was good to have the family all together after their years of separation. Their home was always open, and the children often brought their friends there for hymn singing after the Sunday evening services.

Tommie's sense of humor stayed with him. The family always had a dog, and when Tommie would pass a bone or scrap to it, he'd say, "Buddie, I'd really like to give you an offering, but all I have is a collection."

He'd stir his tea, and then quickly touch the hot spoon to the back of someone's hand.

"As a family we were much the same as others," said Clarence. "We had our share of squabbles as children, but we were always loyal. And Dad never tired of telling about the work of SIM. He gave himself completely to that. The heavier his schedule, the happier he'd be. His great joy was giving. He gave of himself, he gave out the Word, and he gave everything else he had. Dollars never remained long in his pocket. The needs of others and the joy of giving far overshadowed any love for earthly possessions."

When he was home, the children remember always hearing their father's voice after the lights went out, as he and their mother prayed together. They knew their names were included.

When son Emerson was 17 years old, a memorable event took place. "It was one of the proudest days of my life," he recalled. "I'd just come home from school when a registered parcel arrived for mother. I signed for it and took it down to her in the basement where she was busy at the washing machine. I'll never forget the look of amazed unbelief when she realized the significance of that parcel—a gift from the King of England, King George V.

"She shied away from the limelight, for she felt that her labors in Egbe didn't need reward. They were simply an act of love toward the African women and children, an expression of her love for Christ."

The parcel contained a citation and a medal from Buckingham Palace, in recognition of her work at Egbe and the contribution she had made to the welfare of the women and children of that area. What had prompted the process that singled her out is not known, but it is assumed that it all began back in 1922 when the medical officer filed his report to the British Government.

That evening the family examined the medal and citation. It read:

Buckingham Palace
By Command
of
HIS MAJESTY THE KING
to
Ethel Titcombe
to be worn in commemoration of
Their Majesties' Silver Jubilee
6 May, 1935

After 12 years of deputation ministry, Tommie was invited to return to Egbe for the Annual Conference of January 1943. The Second World War was at its height, but Tommie could not refuse. His trip was hazardous, but he arrived safely just before Christmas, for what was undoubtedly one of the highlights of his life. One of the missionaries at Egbe described it in a letter home:

There was great rejoicing when the believers heard that Oyinbo Egbe was on his way. Old Judeti, who had prayed so long for his return, was beside herself with joy, and danced back and forth saying, "When I have seen him again, then my soul shall depart to Heaven."

Weeks passed. Would he arrive for Christmas? Then, on the 22nd, two of us were walking toward the village about five in the afternoon, when we noticed people running—Tommie had come!

By the time we reached the mission, the greetings were well under way, and the porch so crowded we couldn't get through. The black faces were a picture—they registered joyful amazement as they said, "He hasn't grown old!" The younger generation were there, to whom Oyinbo Egbe was a legend; now that they saw him, they stared.

Judeti's legs couldn't keep up with the others who ran after the truck, but she was not far behind. Rather than being hilarious as we expected, she was speechless for joy. The next morning she came back early, and before saluting, prostrated herself in front of the door thanking God for answering her prayers.

Before breakfast was over, the procession began again. It was thrilling to see the old people. There were Sayomi and Danieli, two of the first to believe and suffer for the name of Christ. Another was "Big Peter" and then in striking contrast, Dannie, the dwarf. The old women were not to be outdone. They came in all their glory with a new cloth if they had one, or, if theirs was not good enough, in a borrowed one.

And they brought gifts according to their ability. Some on the heads of their donors, others in their hands, and yet others arrived on their own four legs, led by a rope. The latter were two young calves. Other gifts included ducks, turkeys, roosters, hens, and eggs; then there were bananas, oranges, pawpaw, pineapples and tomatoes.

All exclaimed in wonder and surprise as Mr. Titcombe showed recent pictures of his wife and family. They, too, introduced their children; those Tommie had known, now grown beyond recognition. The chief with his elders, the pastors, teachers and church elders saluted; in fact, most of the town welcomed him.

Tommie sat on the porch greeting the people, and when he retired to his room, some followed him there. His first cook, David, said he broke out in a sweat when he heard Oyinbo Egbe was here, and he walked the 18 miles as fast as he could.

The second evening, Tommie spoke to the Yagba people gathered in the church they had built together. He had been away for twel e years but to the wonder of all, his Yoruba flowed freely. There were at least 1000 within sound of his voice as he spoke on the "Names of Our Lord," so appropriate to the season. The prayers touched my heart, African believers thanked God for bringing back the "father of their faith." The church rang with songs of olden days from hearts overflowing with joy.

At the Christmas service, the choir sang an anthem of welcome and thanks for bringing the gospel to Yagbaland. This had been composed at least two years before, in anticipation and faith that Tommie would return.

There was about a month between the Christmas service and the Annual Conference, during which Tommie made a long tour through the northern part of Nigeria. Then he returned to Egbe for the meetings. When they were over, he reported home:

I have just come from the Yagba conference, and, although all was not accomplished that we would like, we do thank God for what He did, and is going to do yet. . . .

After my messages I gave invitations. A large number responded and stood to show the people—but most of all to show Jesus Christ—that they were ready to follow Him. . . .

It took two hours to gather the special offering on Saturday afternoon. Forty-five churches gave about $3500, and the leaders said the final count will amount to about $5000.

The conference concluded Sunday afternoon with the communion service. Brother Thamer sat at the table and elders passed the bread and wine. As I looked over these men, I noticed two especially. The man who served me came from a village where in 1910 I had to crawl under skulls slung across the path into the village. Now here was a leader from that village serving at the Lord's table, and offering the elements to missionaries.

The second man came from a town where on my first visit I found the priest making a sacrifice to Shango, to bring down rain. Today there are two large churches there, and this elder represented one of them.

Then we stood and sang, "When I Survey the Wondrous Cross." Oh, how real He was to us in that service! There we were, black and white, rejoicing in the glorious privilege of serving Him who loves us.

Tommie had planned on visiting Ethiopia, on the east side of the continent, before heading back home, but he took critically ill and could not go.

After some time in the government hospital in Jos, he wrote home, "Well, I leave the hospital today, almost a miracle. Five days ago they shook their heads and said it was all over for this poor fellow. But they didn't reckon on the Lord, and He sure has answered your prayers for me."

Even in his illness, Tommie remembered Ethel's birthday, and said in his letter, "On the 5th of April will you please send Mrs. Titcombe one dozen roses, as it is her birthday. Charge it to me, and I will repay." No matter where he was, Tommie made sure that a dozen roses greeted Ethel every April 5, sometimes cabled from thousands of miles away.

Back in Canada, Tommie plunged once again into his deputation ministry. Many young people responded to Tommie's challenge. He often took new missionary candidates with him as he traveled, and assisted more than a hundred of them obtain the funds they needed to go to Africa.

He was a guest in many homes, and was always welcomed for his warmth and friendliness and genuine concern. One young woman remembered Tommie's visit to her home:

"My parents often entertained SIM missionaries, and one night my father phoned home, 'I'm bringing Tommie Titcombe home for supper.'

"To my mother, this was like entertaining the King of England. 'Oh!' she said, 'I've just got liver and onions tonight!'

"Well, dad said they'd be home in fifteen minutes anyway, and hung up. When Tommie came he enjoyed the meal so much, and thanked mother over and over for it. 'If people know I'm coming,' he told her, 'they just don't cook liver and onions, and I love them. Thank you. It was a real treat!'"

Psalm 91 remained his favorite all his life. "God has fulfilled every promise in that psalm, one by one, to me personally," he told his audiences.

He had his Bible with him constantly, with passages from Isaiah and the Psalms well marked. "His Bible was his constant companion," said Clarence. "It was beside whatever chair he sat in, it was with him at his bedside, in the car, and everywhere he went."

His faith in God's readiness to answer prayer never wavered. Clarence remembered one time when his mother and father had gone to Canadian Keswick and he was alone. He felt very unwell, and called for help. His lung had collapsed. Friends sent for Tommie and Ethel, who returned immediately.

"As soon as Dad got in the house," said Clarence, "he prayed for me. He was a small man, but he had mountains of faith. Having committed the matter to the Lord, he went about as though his prayer was already answered."

Clarence also remembered the day he took his father to the jewelry store when he bought an engagement ring for his fiancee, Ruth. "Dad," I told him, "my troubles are all over now."

"Don't you believe it, son," he said. "They're just beginning."

During their years of schooling, Tommie often reminded the children that "God is no man's debtor." He wanted them to have the best in education, and taught them, by example as well as by word, to stick with it until they succeeded.

"When I was in medical school," Emerson recalled, "money was pretty scarce at times, and I was embarrassed a little bit to go on my bicycle. I didn't have money for any extras, but dad never let me go without the necessities. He taught me something I never forgot—if you have a worthwhile goal, work hard and you'll reach it."

As Christmas approached each year, the children would watch to see what their father would give to their mother. Tommie always bought his Christmas cards early, and had them addressed and ready for the post box in November. He bought Ethel's gift early, wrapped it beautifully, and hid it. But very often he couldn't stand the excitement of waiting until Christmas Day, so he would bring it out and give it to her ahead of time.

"It was hard for us to see him away from home so much," said Edith, "because even as teenagers we missed him. But we always looked forward to his return, and seeing the pictures and postcards he sent us. And we knew that he was giving his best for the Lord."

Tommie had one last visit to Africa, a nine-month tour of Bible teaching and conference ministry that took him to both sides of the continent, and to Europe on the way home.

The SIM Director for West Africa, Gordon Beacham, invited him because of the needs of the Yagba church. "We are anxious for a spiritual quickening of the churches," he wrote. "We would like you to come in August, and spend several months in a Bible teaching ministry, and conclude with the Annual Conference at Egbe in January. We shall be in prayer for you, for we want only God's will to be done."

Tommie went directly to Egbe, to another emotion-packed reunion. "An ovation was given me of which I am unworthy," he wrote home. "The tears flowed . . . oh, what prayer has brought about in this tribe! One of the first men to greet me this time was just a nine-day-old baby when he was given to me those years ago. Today he is a consecrated young preacher. Yes, one sows, you water, and our Lord gives the increase."

The conference marked the beginning of a foreign missionary outreach for the Yagba church. They had supported evangelists in their own country, but on this occasion were challenged by a missionary from Dahomey to think of those far-away people. Three young men volunteered to go as missionaries, an offering of $150 was taken on the spot, and the young men left with the missionary when conference ended, with the promise of regular financial backing.

"Souls have been saved," Tommie reported, "and Christians brought back into fellowship with the Lord. He has answered your prayers."

The next nine years saw Tommie continue his deputation ministry with increasing effectiveness, although the effects of his relentless service were beginning to tell on him physically.

Many churches look back to a visit from Timmie Titcombe as a turning point in their commitment to world evangelization. The First Congregational Church of Black Rock, in Bridgeport, Connecticut, is one. The church was planning its one hundredth anniversary, and the pastor suggested a missionary conference as part of the celebration.

"They had never had one," said Dr. Cleveland, "and the elders doubted that the people would respond. Finally they agreed for me to select a man who would come for a freewill offering, not a set sum. I invited Tommie.

"The numbers kept growing each night. We took offerings three times for the missionary; they totalled exactly $1000. The people were amazed, and dear Tommie made such an impression that the church has had an annual missionary conference ever since."

So Tommie spent himself, presenting the work of God before the Christian public. Many young people gave their lives to Christ, many found their way into missionary service. Churches and individuals learned to give of their means. Perhaps the reason why God used Tommie so greatly was that he sought nothing for himself.

In the mid-50's he suffered two slight strokes, but rallied and went on. When he could no longer drive his own car, younger men traveled with him.

But the years were catching up with him. At last he reached the point where he realized that he could not continue. He would take some meetings, as he was able, but retirement was inevitable.

19. I will satisfy him

"With a long life I will satisfy him, and let him behold My salvation."
Psalm 91:16

Tommie officially retired in his 78th year, in 1958. At home now with Ethel he felt a growing sense of peace within himself. Now he had more time, time to pray for SIM missionaries by name, for the work, station by station, and for the world.

He kept stationery nearby and continued a lively, hand-written correspondence, encouraging young people and friends in Christian service. He mellowed, Edith observed, but he never lost his zeal for the Lord or for the work of SIM. "He lost his tremendous energy and spontaneity," she said. "He was patient and thoughtful, and slowed down a lot. He often said he was suffering from being born too soon."

Tommie and Ethel had time for relaxation now. They often spent an evening playing parcheesi. "One way or another," Clarence remembered, "Dad always seemed to win, but mother enjoyed the game just as much as he."

Tommie maintained a keen interest in world events, and always listened to the six o'clock news. Every Saturday night he sat by the radio, following the hockey games and cheering enthusiastically for his home team, the Toronto Maple Leafs.

As his sight permitted, he read widely and traveled the world over through the pages of *National Geographic*. He spent more time than ever reading the Word.

Hot tea and fruitcake became an afternoon ritual. Friends stopped by to reminisce and enjoy an hour's fellowship. An even greater treat was to entertain African visitors who found their way to Toronto. Some of these were young church leaders under SIM scholarships, studying for degrees in Canada or the United States. They were happy occasions when someone from Yorubaland, or even Yagbaland, crossed the ocean and entered their home and greeted Oyinbo and Iyawo.

Ethel knew his favorite foods and frequently prepared her special chicken recipe, topping the meal off with elderberry pie. Tommie tended his roses, spending much time with his grandson and namesake Tommy, who lived nearby. In season, he would choose the most perfect rosebud each day to take to Ethel; should there be a lady guest, he'd cut another.

By June of 1965 Tommie, still bright and happy, although increasingly aware of the limited time he had left, spoke frequently of his departure for heaven. He wrote to some friends of many years:

I have been much interested in your Bible Evangelism work and I sure do praise the Lord for all He is doing for you and through you. In these days of apostasy, when so many unconverted preachers are just preaching everything *but* the gospel, how refreshing it is to know that there are those like yourself preaching, "Thus saith the Lord."

Now as for your friend Tommie, he is just about at the end of the road and will soon be with Him, which is far better. My eyes are getting dim; I am quite deaf, my blood pressure is high, and my heart weak. My hands are crippled with arthritis, but apart from that, I am just fine!

God bless you, dear ones. I'm praying for you. Your aged friend, 84 years young, Tommie.

Early on the morning of November 22, 1965, Ethel woke Tommie.

"Well, Dad," she smiled, "we made it!" It was their 50th wedding anniversary, a happy day that was spent with family and friends.

Tommie and Ethel relished life in their cozy red-brick bungalow in north Toronto, and were reluctant to leave it. But in 1967 they moved to Shepherd Lodge, a Christian retirement home in the city. They adjusted to this new way of life, and appreciated the care they received and the friendship of others of their age. What affected Tommie most was the feeling of being away from SIM. "Dad felt lonely during that year," said Emerson. "He felt cut off from SIM except through correspondence and a few faithful visitors. He frequently remarked about this."

Occasionally they visited their sons, who lived in the Toronto area. Edith and her husband lived too far away, in Richmond, Virginia.

"No matter whether the weather was ten below zero or ninety-five above," Clarence remembered, "Dad always wore his hat, collar, and tie when he came to see us. If he spent the night, his last joke would be about his teeth being like the stars—they come out at night!"

On his last visit to Emerson's family, Tommie made the effort to speak for a few minutes at the church. "I feared he wouldn't make it," said Emerson. "But as I introduced him, I could read his deep appreciation in his eyes. He literally lived in the lives of his children."

In the months preceding Tommie's death, if Emerson asked him how he felt, Tommie would reply quietly, "Son, I'm awful tired. I just want to go Home."

Then one day he did. On May 29, 1968, at the age of 87, Tommie slipped away to meet many of his beloved Yagbas, a part of the great family of faith, forever present with the Lord.

Two of the pallbearers at the funeral were Nigerian pastors, one of them from near the town of Egbe. On behalf of his Yoruba people, pastor Moses Durojaiye gave thanks for the service of the white man, Oyinbo Egbe, who had taken the gospel to the Yagba people 50 years before.

"It was the completion of a cycle," Edith observed. "Dad had ministered in his lifetime in Africa, and at the end of his life, Africans ministered to him."

Ethel continued living at Shepherd Lodge, lonesome for Tommie, but contented and in good health. She liked to reminisce about the women and children of Egbe.

"She always looked so nice," said one of her friends, who visited her several times. "Her hair was done beautifully, she wore a nice dress, and sat in her rocking chair like a royal lady—which she was! With tears in her eyes and a lovely smile she would tell me, 'I'm so glad the Lord sent me to Egbe. Just think, He sent *me*!'

"One day she took a picture of Tommie out of a drawer to show me. It was a typical photo, a good one, showing that grin and the twinkle in his eye. 'I've tried leaving this out on my table,' she told me, 'but I just haven't been able to bear it. I miss him so much.'

"The next time I visited, though, it was on the table, and it stayed there until she went to the hospital."

What sent her to the hospital was a fall that fractured her hip and shoulder. She never really rallied.

On Sunday, February 15, 1970, Ethel Titcombe slipped quietly away to the Father's house, to be with her beloved Tommie, at the feet of Jesus.

20. Tommie has the last word

"The Teacher is here, and is calling for you." John 11:28
(Excerpted from a message Tommie gave to an audience of 3000 at English Keswick.)

On a Saturday morning years ago, here in this place, a young American student spoke for five or six minutes. Out of that brief address the Student Volunteer Movement began. One recognizes that the greatest events of the Christian world do not come from much talking or dramatic preparation; they come when men adjust to God's plans.

Had Mr. Wilder spoken the year before, or even some days earlier, the student movement might not have happened. But a band of students from the Scottish and English universities had been prepared by attendance at that Keswick Convention for the challenge he brought.

That is why one would like to think that here, at the close of this Convention, there have been adjustments made, conditioning you to respond to the appeal of God and the world.

J

When I look on this gathering of young, prepared lives and then on the world, I cannot help hearing the call of God to every soul here, demanding your life.

I feel as Francis Xavier did. He wanted to go through the universities of Europe crying, "O men, what a multitude of souls are lost through your neglect!"

What God wants today, and what the world needs, is for you and me to recognize that we are not called to individual service, or to national service, but to worldwide service—to make Jesus Christ King in lives for whom He died. God requires that you "present your bodies a living and holy sacrifice"; then you will know the joy of sacrifice, when you recognize that all you have is too little to offer in response to what Christ did for you.

I recently read the story of a concert in a prison in America. There, they had been using modern methods for the entertainment and reform of the prisoners. The prisoners formed an orchestra and choir, and one evening these groups broadcast to the outside world.

They played and sang the great pieces of master composers, and for an hour those souls in prison burst through their granite walls, soared through the night, and sang their song in the homes of villages and cities in America.

Men and women, we have a song—the song of Christ and His redemption, and we want to share it until hearts around the world can sing it with us.

I speak to young men and women here who have prepared, cultured lives to give to God. Is He asking you to give Him your best? What will your motive be? I am not going to press one of you, out of the excitement of the moment, to give yourself to be a missionary, but I do ask you to consider two compelling motives that must send us into the mission field: the need of the world, and the need of Jesus Christ.

I've heard Christians say, "But the world doesn't want us today." The whole story of missions is the story of offering to people a gift they do not desire. My plea is not that the world *wants* us, but that the world *needs* us. We *must* be missionaries, when we realize that by taking God's gift to a lost world, we can bring it to Christ. My strongest plea is that we must be missionaries to truly explain the love of Christ.

"For God so loved the world, that he gave his only begotten Son, that whosoever believeth in him should not perish, but have everlasting life." In the light of John 3:16, I cannot truly interpret the cross until I see that love is not a limited, narrow, trickling stream passing between high banks of color and national prejudice, but is like the sea, fathomless, limitless, in which all humanity may bathe. It is because Jesus Christ has delivered me, that I believe He can deliver anybody who comes to Him. He is the Savior of the world!

Now if you believe this, what is your response? Two ways are open to you: toil, with sure triumph, or ease, with safe disgrace. I had rather spend one month burning out for God in Asia or Africa, than a long life of comfort here at home.

I have a Greek New Testament, given to me by Canon Gardiner after a meeting here at Keswick. On the flyleaf is written: "The measure of our agony is the measure of our success."

A few years ago, in an early morning talk with students out there on the lake, with the sun shining overhead, the water calm as glass, and the birds singing in the trees, Mr. Stewart of Fukien, China, speaking of the agony of Christ in Gethsemane, said: "Gentlemen, you will measure your life not by the wine drunk, but by the wine poured forth, and the measure of your agony will be the measure of your success." Within a year, Stewart and his party were massacred. One may say, "What a waste of life!"

I say, "What a glorious harvest has come out of that grain planted in the name of the Lord!"

You may have the privilege of following where they led; of filling up the vacancies that exist today all over the world.

There is a story told by Mason, in his book *Running Water*, of how the message of a disaster on the mountainside came to guides in an Alpine village. Immediately, these men arose from their supper tables, took lanterns, axes, and ropes, and went to the rescue. They knew that some of them might die, for, he wrote, "There is a law among the guides, the last to be broken, that what a man knows, he must do, if by doing it he may save a life."

There is a law in Christian service, the last to be broken, that what a man knows, that he must do, if by doing it, he may save a life!

Apply this law today. If you know that Jesus Christ died for the sins of the world, and that He is able to save to the uttermost those who come to Him, then there is a law you must not break. You *must* dedicate your life to this most glorious service.

Give yourself to God, that out of your service, whether long or short, some light may break on people still in darkness, and some glory come to Christ our Lord.

PART FOUR
Tommie's dream realized

The Yoruba scene today

"O magnify the Lord with me, and let us exalt His name together."
Psalm 34:3

The Yoruba tribe, numbering more than ten million, lives in the western region of Nigeria between the Niger River and the Atlantic Ocean and spills over into Dahomey.

Yoruba young people are growing up in the "Third World" with education available at all levels. In Ibadan, the largest "African" city on the continent (population 750,000), the University College boasts a fine Medical School complete with a teaching hospital, where students may receive training to become doctors, nurses and paramedics. Degrees in the other professions are also available. The University of Ife and Lagos University are also degree-granting schools in this region.

A. *The Church then and today*

When Tommie arrived in Egbe with David Adeniyi, the little boy chosen by the Ogga church to help him, he was "all things to all men." He gossiped the gospel as fast and as simply as he could master the language. "And the Lord was adding to their number day by day those who were being saved" (Acts 2:47). Tommie's right-hand man, David, put it this way: "The Word of God gained ground very fast at Egbe, due mainly to the assistance he [Tommie] gave to the poor people, who were being persecuted by the chiefs and other men of influence. This made the gospel work heavy and excessive until another missionary was brought for assistance."

The believers gathered under shade trees at first; were baptized, and erected simple churches. It was a small beginning but now, 65 years later, there are 107 congregations in the Yoruba area. These SIM-affiliated churches are members of the Evangelical Churches of West Africa, support their own work and also stand behind young couples serving as missionaries under ECWA's Evangelical Missionary Society.

The church at Egbe seats more than 1000. They have an average of 960 attending each week, with 400 on the church roll. The Sunday School averages more than 560 a Sunday.

Preaching teams go out to surrounding towns and villages with encouraging results.

B. *Education then and today*

David of Ogga and Aliyu of Egbe, who helped Tommie learn the Yoruba language, were his first pupils. Soon he started a day school, then six years later, a boarding school. As the work grew, the Mission opened schools in the district including elementary, secondary, orphanages, girl's schools, teacher's colleges and a degree-granting seminary. The ECWA church has turned over the 37 elementary schools in Yorubaland to the Local Education Authorities.

Titcombe College at Egbe, named to honor the one who began the work there, opened as a high school in 1951. In 1956, the first 13 students graduated with a High School Certificate. Girls were first admitted in 1966. In 1971, 62 graduated, making a total of 714.

Then the school added a five-year West Africa School Certificate course, equivalent to junior college in the States. By 1971, 213 had received their diplomas in the college section.

An interesting analysis of Titcombe College graduates who went on to obtain higher degrees was compiled in 1972:

Post Graduate Courses	Overseas	Where			In Nigeria	Total
medical doctors	10	U.K.	U.S.A.	Australia	15	25
veterinarians	4	"			5	9
teachers (B.A. & M.A.)	40	"	"		160	200
engineers	12	"	"	U.S.S.R.	80	92
administrators	6	"	"	France	40	46
diplomats	2	"		"	6	8
architects	3	"			5	8
electronics eng. (Ph. D.)	1					1
theologians	1		"		6	7
military personnel	18		"	" U.S.S.R.,	50	68
(inc. pilots)		West Germany, Canada				
lawyers					1	1
Total	97				368	465

Today five post-elementary schools are staffed by qualified Yoruba principals and teachers. Many Christian teachers are employed in the mission-oriented elementary schools now operated by the government.

C. *Medicine then and today*

Before Tommie's arrival, the sick went to the medicine man. An early diary reveals a glimpse of Tommie's medical work: "set a broken leg today"; "operated on a sick man, cut off toe"; "pulled out two teeth this morning." "Medical work" was the first entry almost every day. We see this ministry through David Adeniyi's eyes: "Rev. Titcombe had so much compassion for the poor that he would not overlook anyone in sickness. Much as he was not a doctor, he would cure sores and all other types of disease. He almost turned himself into a doctor."

When Tommie brought Ethel to Egbe as his bride in December 1915, a new chapter began two days after her arrival, with the saving of the lives of the first pair of twins. Ethel developed a large, effective maternity work and carried it on, without any formal training, until 1927, when the first doctor and registered nurse were appointed to Egbe.

Through the years, SIM opened dispensaries at its stations in the Yoruba area, also two leprosaria and the hospital at Egbe. From such a humble beginning in 1908, the report now reads that Egbe Hospital has 104 beds with 2 doctors, 27 nurses and a staff of 114. In 1971, 80,546 patients received treatment; 716 major and 1206 minor surgical operations were performed, also 484 deliveries. The outpatient depart-

K

ment treated an average of 260 a day. One hundred and seventeen nurses received their R.N. after training there. The Hospital phased out this course in 1971 and introduced a Community Nurses Training School. By 1972, 30 students had enrolled.

The hospital employs three full-time pastors who conduct daily services in the wards and out-patient department. They also counsel each patient individually before discharge.

In addition, 23 from the Yoruba area have graduated from the SIMMATS (SIM Medical Auxiliaries Training School) program at Evangel Hospital in Jos, Northern Nigeria.

D. *Mass media today in Yorubaland*

1. *The African Challenge*, a monthly magazine published in English since 1951, reached a circulation of more than 150,000, with a bi-monthly Yoruba edition of 65,000 copies, before being replaced at the end of 1973 by *Today's Challenge*.

It is noteworthy that the General Manager, Rev. James Bolarin, comes from the Egbe area.

2. *Radio*. When Tommie began at Egbe, the fastest means of communication was the talking drum. When he visited the villages, one town would send news of his coming by drumbeat to the next village along the trail.

Tommie didn't need a public address system. He could preach to crowds of a thousand or more, for God gave him a built-in P.A. system.

But how thrilled he was when SIM's radio voice, Radio Station ELWA, Monrovia, Liberia, went on the air in 1954. Soon after, with the installation of the first shortwave transmitter, his beloved Yoruba people began to hear programs in their language, beamed from ELWA and picked up on small transistor radios.

At first, missionaries recorded messages by Yoruba pastors and evangelists and airmailed them to ELWA. But since 1955, the Igbaja Recording Studio with trained Yoruba staff has produced tapes of professional quality for ELWA to broadcast to the Yoruba nation. Rev. David Olatayo, the director, is an ordained ECWA minister with a B.R.E. degree from Central Baptist Seminary in Toronto, Canada. He also prepares taped messages in English for Nigerian programs.

But the story isn't all told yet. God continues to call out a people for His name in Yorubaland, and is choosing and training national leaders to move into leadership.

One of these dedicated men shared his concern for the future: "We must maintain high spiritual principles, and we need qualified personnel and finances to keep up present standards."

When asked how interested Christians abroad might help the Yoruba church, he urged that we pray:

1. For church leaders, that they will teach their people the Scriptures in depth and emphasize personal systematic Bible study.
2. For the establishment of strong ECWA churches in the big cities.
3. For a vigorous program for youth, women and children.
4. For the outreach through mass media.

In conclusion he stressed again the key to it all—that the Yoruba church must have spiritual leaders whom God will use to rouse individual believers to resist materialism and live a separated life. Tommie had a great God and he dreamed great things for his beloved Yoruba people.

God will honor his faith!

Glossary

animist—a person who believes that natural phenomena and objects, as rocks, trees, the wind, etc., are alive and have souls

cowrie shells—the shell of a certain sea animal usually fastened together in strings of 40 or 100 each, used as currency. Imported from the East Indies. 150 cowries = 1 cent. (40 cowries = 1 string; 50 strings = 1 head; 10 heads = 1 bag.)

demon possession—a person having yielded himself to be possessed by a devil or evil spirit

dowry—traditionally, "the bridegroom-elect had to present to the parents of the intended bride, choice kola-nuts, some alligator pepper, and bitter kolas. Also a fine wrapper of good quality, a large covering cloth, a head tie, and some money according to his ability. In animistic families, the parties themselves had to carry special propitiatory sacrifices offered to the evil one. This is termed *Ebo Iyawa* (A bride's sacrifice.) From *History of the Yorubas*, Johnson, p. 114.

Egungun—the worship of the departed spirits of ancestors

Esu—the devil, Satan

Fulani—migrated from Upper Egypt, entered Nigeria in 13th century. Some lived in towns, others retained their pastoral habits.

Hausa—a nation in northern Nigeria made up originally of seven states. The Hausa language is the *lingua franca* of a large part of West Africa. (*History of Nigeria*, Burns, p. 41.)

Igbomina—a sub-tribe of the Yoruba nation

Igunnu—god of motherhood

Iyawo—bride

lorry—truck

Muhammad—founder of the Islamic religion (570–632 A.D.)

Muslim—a follower of the prophet Muhammad

mouth friend—insincere friend

my stomach is sweet—I feel happy

Nupe—an Islamic emirate under Sarkin Musulmi, who lived in Sokoto

Ogun—god of war and all things made of iron

"Oku, Baba."—"Greetings, father."

Olorun—the Lord of the Heavens

126

Omo Egbe—child of Egbe
Osain—god of sickness and health
Oyinbo—"man of the peeled skin," white man
Oyinbo Egbe—white man of Egbe
pan roof—roof made of sheets of galvanized iron roofing
polygamy—the state of having two or more wives at the same time
Shango—god of thunder and lightning (also *Sango*)
umbrella hat—an umbrella-sized hat made of leaves
water baby—traditionally the newborn baby was fed only medicinal water the first nine days—85% died.
Yagba—an agricultural sub-tribe of the Yoruba nation

Chronology of the life of Tommie Titcombe

1881   September 17: Tommie born, Swindon, Wiltshire, England, son of George and Sarah Titcombe.
1902   At age 21 completes apprenticeship as a molder at the Great Western Railway in Swindon.
       Is converted to Christ at Railway Mission.
1903   Goes to Canada with two friends. Settles in Hamilton, Ontario. Joins the Gospel Tabernacle.
1906   Thanksgiving Day, hears missionary from Nigeria, dedicates his life. Immediately arranges interview with Rev. R. V. Bingham, Director of SIM, is turned down for service, but is given course of training to follow.
       Two weeks later enters the Missionary Training Institute in New York City.
1908   May: Graduates from Missionary Training Institute.
       Mr. Bingham turns him down again. As Tommie is determined to go to Africa, Pastor Philpott and people at Gospel Tabernacle promise to stand behind him. SIM accepts him.
       Tommie hears furloughing missionary Lang tell of Yagba believers praying for a missionary.
       July: Leaves Canada with George Sanderson for Africa, via England.
       September: Arrives in Nigeria.
       October: Nine-year old Osanyigbemi Adeniyi (David) of Ogga is given to Tommie.
       November: Tommie and David go to Egbe to begin work among Yagba people.
       Christmas Day: Alone with David and sick with malaria at Egbe.
1909   May: Preaches first sermon in Yagba in Egbe market.
       October 31: First Baptismal service in SIM. Ten men and three women baptized in Ogga (including little David).
       Fred Rutherford joins Tommie at Egbe.
       New Year's Eve: First watchnight service is held at Ogga.
1910   New Year's Day: Tommie claims Jeremiah 33:3 for Yagba work.

February: Revival begins at Egbe. Tommie moves into his own house in town.

April: Eleven believers at Egbe.

May 29: Largest crowds to date. 100 decisions for Christ. Evening service—800.

Tommie treks often to villages during the year.

1911 Two hundred and fifty learn to read their Bibles before Tommie goes on furlough.

July: Tommie goes on furlough.

August: Guy Playfair arrives on field. Is stationed with Fred Rutherford at Egbe.

1912 January: Mr. Rutherford is invalided home.

April: Tommie arrives back at Egbe.

June: Mr. Rutherford dies in London, Ontario.

November: First Baptism at Egbe. Ninety-nine (83 men and 16 women).

Guy Playfair opens new station at Oro.

1913 Now 20 churches in Yagbaland.

November: 116 are baptized at Egbe (82 men and 34 women).

1914 January 1: Nigeria is unified as The Colony and Protectorate of Nigeria with Lord Lugard as Governor-General.

May: Starts Sunday School with 375 attending.

October: Government order requires Tommie move outside town. He appeals.

December: Mr. Bingham and party, including Miss Ethel McIntosh, Tommie's fiancee, arrive in Nigeria. Rev. Norman Davis is appointed to Egbe.

1915 New Year's Day: Mr. Bingham and Mr. Mackenzie visit Egbe. First Annual Yagba Conference. 100 are baptized.

Christians complete new church.

Rev. A. W. Banfield visits Egbe.

Drought. God sends rain in answer to prayers of Christians.

Tommie's appeal is refused. He builds small house on edge of town for his bride.

November 22: Tommie and Ethel marry in Minna.

December 23: They arrive at Egbe.

Christmas Day: Ethel saves the lives of the first pair of twins to live in Yagbaland.

1916 Fourteen out-stations are listed under Egbe with an average attendance of 1535.

Two hundred Bibles are sold during the year.

1917 December 15: Clarence Herbert Titcombe is born at Egbe—first white child born in Yagbaland.

1918 August: The Titcombes leave for furlough.

1919   March 29: Twins, Edith and Emerson, are born in Hamilton, Ontario.
        December: Tommie sails for Nigeria alone.
1920   February: Tommie arrives back at Egbe.
        Tommie builds maternity center and works with Christians on their new church.
        August: Ethel and the three children arrive at Egbe.
1921   June 5: New church dedicated, debt-free. Nineteen out-stations are listed under Egbe with 2025 adherents. Eight evangelists.
        New school building is erected with Yoruba teacher in charge.
1922   July 10: Chief Medical Officer at Ilorin inspects the new maternity center. Twenty-two out-stations are listed with 2600 adherents.
1923   April: Titcombes leave on furlough.
1924   September: Mr. and Mrs. Titcombe leave the three children in Canada.
        October: Arrive back at Egbe.
1925   New 40-bed maternity hospital is completed at Egbe.
        David Adeniyi begins to teach at Egbe.
        Twenty-seven young men go to Bible School from Egbe.
1926   July: Mrs. Titcombe is invalided home to Canada.
1927   June: Tommie goes on furlough.
        David Adeniyi becomes pastor of Egbe Church.
        Miss Margaret Lang, R.N., is first trained nurse appointed to Egbe.
        Dr. Harry Peaston, M.B.Ch.B., L.R.C.P., is appointed to Egbe hospital.
1929   July: Tommie arrives back at Egbe.
1930   August: Tommie becomes ill, goes on furlough. He does not return to Nigeria, except for two visits.
        Tommie becomes SIM Representative in North America.
1935   Ethel receives decoration from King George V for her work with African twins.
1942-43 Tommie visits Nigeria from Dec. 1942–May 1943.
1943   Tommie is busy in SIM Jubilee (1893–1943) meetings.
1948-49 Tommie revisits Nigeria from August 1948–January 1949.
        Flies to East Africa with Mr. Playfair and Dr. and Mrs. Darroch and on to Great Britain for speaking engagements.
1949   Full schedule in USA and Canada.
1951   Titcombe College is established at Egbe.
1958   December: Tommie retires in 78th year. Attends SIM Council meetings and speaks at Conferences as long as able.
1965   Is hospitalized. Heart attacks begin causing great pain.
1966   Tommie retires from Canadian Council of SIM.
1967   April: The Titcombes move to Shepherd Lodge, Toronto.
1968   May 29: Tommie dies in Toronto, Canada.
1970   February 15: Ethel dies in Toronto, Canada.

Bibliography

1. Books

Ben Yahmed, Bechir *Africa 69/70*. Paris: Jeune Afrique, 1969.

Bingham, Rowland V. *Seven Sevens of Years and a Jubilee*. Toronto: Evangelical Publishers, 1943.

Bulifant, Josephine C. *Forty Years in the African Bush*. Grand Rapids: Zondervan Publishing House, 1950.

Burns, Sir Alan. *History of Nigeria*. London: George Allen and Unwin, Ltd., 4th Ed., 1948.

Darroch, M. A. *How Shall They Hear?* Grand Rapids: Zondervan Publishing House, 1958.

Davidson, Basil. *The African Past*. London: Penguin Books, Ltd., 1966.

Davidson, Basil. *Black Mother*. London: Victor Gollancz, Ltd., 1961.

Davidson, Basil. *The Growth of African Civilization: A History of West Africa, 1000-1800*. London: Longmans, 1969 (reprint).

Fuja, Abayomi. *Fourteen Hundred Cowries*. (Traditional Stories of the Yoruba). Ibadan: Oxford University Press, 1962.

Fuller, W. Harold. *Run While the Sun Is Hot*. Toronto: Sudan Interior Mission.

Hodder, B. W. and Ukwu, U. I. *Markets in West Africa*. Ibadan: Ibadan University Press, 1969.

Hunter, James H. *A Flame of Fire*. Toronto: Sudan Interior Mission, 1961.

Huxley, Elspeth. *Four Guineas*. A Journey Through West Africa. London: Chatto and Windus, 1957.

Johnson, Rev. Samuel. *The History of the Yorubas*. Lagos: C. M. S. Bookshop, 1937.

Livingstone, W. P. *Mary Slessor*. N.Y.: George H. Doran Co., 8th Ed.

Lucas, J. Olumide. *The Religion of the Yorubas*. Lagos: C. M. S. Bookshop, 1948.

Percy, Douglas C. *Doctor to Africa*. Toronto: Sudan Interior Mission, 1948.

Phillips, Arthur. *Survey of African Marriage and Family Life*. London: Oxford University Press, 1953.

Seligman, C. G. *Races of Africa*. London: Oxford University Press. 3rd ed. 1957.

Smith, Edwin W. *African Ideas of God*. London: Edinburgh House Press, 1950.

Stewart, James, *Dawn in the Dark Continent*. Edinburgh: Oliphant, Anderson and Ferrier, 1906.

Tucker, Miss *Abeokuta; or Sunrise Within the Tropics*. London: James Nesbit and Co., 2nd Ed. 1853.

Underwood, Leon. *Masks of West Africa*. London: Alec. Tiranti, Ltd., 1952.

Underwood, Leon. *Figures in Wood of West Africa*. London: Alec. Tiranti, Ltd., 1951.

Webster, J. B. and Boahen, A. A. *The Growth of African Civilization: The Revolutionary Years, West Africa Since 1800*. London: Longmans, 1970 (5th impression).

2. Booklets

Adeniyi, D. O. *How Christianity Was Introduced Into Yagba and Igbomina Lands*. Egbe: Oluwalomehin-Ola Press.

SIM Annual Reports

3. Magazine Articles

Many excerpts from articles printed in *Faithful Witness*, from March 6, 1900; magazine name changed to *Missionary Witness* by 1904; name changed again to *Evangelical Christian* by 1919.

Bolarin, James K. "History and Ministry of Challenge," *African Challenge*, No. 235, 6.

Lovering, Kerry. "Egbe Pioneer Passes," *Africa Now*, (July-August, 1968) 13.

Emenyonu, Ernest and Pat. "The Writer and His World: Achebe: Accountable to our society" *Africa Report*, May 1972, 21.

Index